ED RANDOLPH

AUTHOR OF *SMOKED*

SHOWSTOPPING BBQ
– *with your* –
TRAEGER® GRILL

STANDOUT RECIPES *for your* WOOD PELLET COOKER
from an AWARD-WINNING PITMASTER

PAGE STREET
PUBLISHING CO.

PAGE STREET
PUBLISHING CO.

I would like to dedicate this book to my wife Noelle.

From the beginning you have taught me that happiness is a choice and everything else is a matter of perspective. You have encouraged me, believed in me and pushed me to follow my dreams. You've taught me to be captivated by my purpose and not distracted by comparison. You make me want to do my best, be my best and improve constantly. I love you, Mena.

Life isn't about waiting for the storm to pass. It's about learning to dance in the rain.

Contents

FOREWORD

The reemergence of barbecue on the American food scene during the past ten years has been an explosive, wildly fun ride. Outside of the South and traditional barbecue strongholds like Texas and Kansas City, barbecue was a verb. It was something you did, not something you ate. Flip the calendar not too far back and the joys of peppery brisket, vinegary pork and white-sauced chicken were only to be found in their natural habitats or were spoken about outside their territorial boundaries only in whispers. Most of the country was unaware of and very few of us had access to these wonders. Tell someone you are a competitive barbecue cook these days and you're likely to become engaged in a conversation about the nuances of eastern versus western Carolina sauces. The Internet and the spread of social media certainly had a big part in breaking down those boundaries, but so did the new legions of pitmasters who came from areas outside of the traditional strongholds—pitmasters like Ed Randolph.

I'm not exactly sure where I first met Ed, but I am willing to bet it was far from home. For years we crossed paths on the competitive barbecue trail and despite being neighbors in the Hudson Valley, we never had time to sit down and have a beer at home. Knowing our shared love of beef, bourbon and Barolo, that may be a blessing in disguise. We have said more than once that if that love were allowed to prosper it might get us into trouble.

Who is Ed? Ed is the quiet guy in the back with the bright eyes and sly smile. Ed is the guy hustling, leading the Handsome Devil team to festivals and contests up and down the East Coast. I mention hustle because that is his motto, his driving force, the ethos he lives by each and every day. Hustle—it is yours for the taking, you just have to go out and grab it. It is an ideal that we both share. Ed is the guy winning *Chopped*, winning "Best BBQ" at the Food Network's New York Wine & Food Festival or walking the stage at Harpoon. Ed is the guy serving a perfectly cooked whole hog, an entire steamship round or . . . wait, hold on a second, is that an alligator coming out of the smoker? Is that an octopus in its mouth? Yup, that, ladies and gentlemen, is my friend Ed.

I have watched as the Handsome Devil LLC team has become one of the most instantly recognizable names on the barbecue festival trail. One of the things that immediately stood out to me about Handsome Devil was the organization, presentation and showmanship that the entire team exuded. Confident but not cocky, the HD team continues to wow people with their own brand of hospitality. A native of New York's Hudson Valley, Ed is not beholden to conventional wisdom or tied to age-old traditions. He has put in thousands of miles and countless hours learning the tried-and-true techniques of the ancient masters, but he is not afraid to go outside the box and give us something new. He has thrown his hat into the ring with the big boys and girls of the barbecue world and not only held his own but shown us a glimpse into the future and what is possible.

The word is out on what good barbecue truly is, and technology is making it accessible for just about anyone. Pellet cookers have leveled the playing field in so many ways. They have allowed the everyday cook, the novice, the once-in-a-while griller to make food they would not otherwise be able to. Today's pellet cookers offer cooks an unprecedented ability to produce world-class brisket, yet they are versatile machines that can do so much more. In today's fast-paced world, not everyone has time to sit and tend a fire between work, soccer games, football practice and dance lessons. A pellet cooker may not give you that sense of caveman therapy by playing with a fire, but it will give you a chance to drop Jimmy at his buddy's house and Susie at piano and still have time to sit on the patio and allow you to enjoy a cocktail while you finish up those St. Louis spares with smoked scalloped potatoes.

Ed has a knack for making the difficult appear easy, and his depth of knowledge combined with his flair for the new and innovative come together perfectly in this book, guiding us through a wide-open new world of live-fire cooking, where we can sear, smoke, bake and roast just about any recipe we can cook up.

Old-school stick burners I'm sure will take umbrage and say we're cheating, but so be it. The hell with the old dogs not wanting to learn new tricks. It's a bright, brazen new world, so come sit down and enjoy a bourbon with us and let Ed show you how easy it can be.

—SEAN KEEVER,
Big Guns BBQ

INTRODUCTION

About ten years ago I attended a course led by an esteemed chef of the Culinary Institute, and at one point he explained the difference between barbecue and grilling. Grilling is at high heat over an open flame, while barbecuing is traditionally done at low temperatures over long periods of time. I couldn't disagree with the chef's descriptions; however, to me, barbecue is so much more than just slow and low temperatures. It's about family, friends and the memories made together. When I show up at someone's party and I am intrigued by the tempting smell of smoke in the air, I'm in my happy place. I know someone spent time sharing their passion with me and the other guests. Learning to barbecue is a process, and I am sorry to tell you that no book, not even this one, will facilitate that knowledge overnight. It takes time and patience.

However, if this book caught your attention, then it is safe to assume you are a barbecue aficionado who is dedicated and wants to learn more about the craft. And so let me introduce you to the Traeger® grill, among the best grills for your dollar in today's market. It is simple to use and the wood pellets let you get phenomenal results immediately. With some practice, you will start to realize the versatility that the Traeger grill can offer and will find yourself becoming worthy of the title "pitmaster."

What makes me think I can help you? Well, I was you. When I started my barbecue journey, I purchased an offset, a ceramic cooker and a pellet smoker/grill. Each offers different characteristics; however, the more I used the pellet smoker, the more I was impressed. Soon I found myself taking it to Kansas City Barbecue Society (KCBS) competitions. As the years went on and my business grew, so did my cooking capacity needs, so I upgraded to larger commercial cookers. My company, Handsome Devil LLC, now provides barbecue concessions and catering at some of the largest events from Vermont to Florida. We have KCBS championship awards in six states, have won Food Network's New York City Wine & Food Festival (NYCWFF) and I won a little show called *Chopped*. I also authored *Smoked: One Man's Journey to Find Incredible Recipes, Standout Pitmasters and the Stories Behind Them*. However, even with all that travel, I still have my Traeger Lil' Tex Elite on my back porch.

Traeger is one of the most versatile cookers on the market. It can smoke, it can grill and it can bake, all with a turn of the dial. The pellet varieties allow you to achieve the same flavor profile as if you were using firewood. The only difference is the pellets are a guaranteed hardwood that burn clean and for a long time. This provides consistency in your cooking and helps you develop the skills to become a professional pitmaster.

I can't stress enough the importance of practice. Barbecue takes time. Achieving the best results is a long, time-consuming process. There is no crash course or cheat sheet that can explain how to master making a brisket. It comes down to you and your smoker working together to achieve that perfect, tender slice. The good news is that the practice to find that perfection is as delicious as reaching the goal. The memories made with your friends and family will be something you can cherish.

BASIC TRAEGER KNOW-HOW

So you've heard of gas grills and charcoal grills, but what is this you keep hearing about pellet grills? What are pellet grills? How do these grills work? And, more important, are pellet grills the right grill for you?

Pellet grills, sometimes referred to as pellet smokers, are outdoor cookers that combine elements of charcoal smokers, gas grills and kitchen ovens. Fueled by wood pellets, they can smoke, grill and bake. Joe Traeger developed and patented the Traeger pellet grill in the mid-1980s and began production in 1988. Traeger grills have a side-mounted pellet hopper and a rotating auger that feeds pellets from the hopper to the fire pot, where they are lit by an igniter. An induction fan then stokes the fire and distributes heat and smoke throughout the grill. A deflector plate sits between the fire and the grill grate, keeping food and grease from coming into contact with the fire.

A Traeger pellet grill plugs into a standard 15-amp electrical outlet and burns hardwood pellets. The controller monitors the temperature inside the grill and automatically feeds more or fewer pellets into the fire pot to maintain the selected temperature setting.

Above and beyond the obvious difference in fuel type (wood pellets versus propane versus charcoal), a pellet grill differs from the others in three ways: peace of mind, consistent cooking and usefulness. With a Traeger grill, you don't have to stand over a fire and babysit. Instead, you can set the heat and let your Traeger do the rest. This cuts out the time you need for purchasing additional supplies and nursing charcoal briquettes or adjusting the flames on a gas grill. It's easier to use than a kitchen appliance. Next, it is a proven fact that consistent temperature will give you consistent results. A Traeger pellet grill delivers the most consistent flavor of any grill. Finally, it is the versatility of a Traeger grill that is one of its defining features. Along with its steak-searing capabilities and slow-smoking attributes, it also acts as a moisture-rich oven for baking great homemade pizzas, bread and assorted casseroles. Even your twenty-pound (9-kg) family Thanksgiving turkey will taste better cooked on a Traeger grill.

Now that you know a little about Traeger pellet grills, let me tell you how to get it ready for cooking. Depending on which Traeger grill you purchase, there may be some minor assembly required. Don't worry, a mechanical engineering degree is not required. All you need are a couple of open-end wrenches, a hex key and a screwdriver to complete the assembly. Please refer to the owner's manual for your specific Traeger model for installation instructions.

Starting your Traeger couldn't be any easier than the push of a button. Depending on which Traeger model you purchase, it will come equipped with either the Digital Pro Controller or the Traeger WiFIRE® Electronic Controller. For those with the Digital Pro Controller, you will want to open the grill door, turn the switch to ON and the temperature dial to SMOKE. After two minutes, you will notice the pellets start to ignite and a white smoke will come out of the grill. At this time you can close the door and turn the temperature dial to your desired setting. For those with the WiFIRE controller, make sure the main power switch is turned on, and then press the STANDBY button to awaken the grill display. Your grill's home screen defaults to the "Turn Dial to Select Temperature" message. You can select your cooking temperature directly from this screen. Turn the selector knob right or left to your desired temperature, and then press the center of the dial to select your temperature. Press the IGNITE button and your Traeger will start the automatic preheat cycle. Allow your Traeger to preheat for about 10 minutes with the door closed before putting any food on the grill grate.

Regardless of the Traeger you own, it is important that you shut down your grill properly when your cook is complete. For those with the digital controller, turn the selector knob to the SHUT DOWN cycle. For those with the WiFIRE controller, press and hold the STANDBY button to get to the shut down screen.

Types of Pellets

Traeger offers a variety of wood pellets to use in their grills. All are made from 100 percent natural, food-grade hardwood that will burn clean and provide an optimal wood-fired flavor.

PELLET TYPE	DESCRIPTION	RECOMMENDED COOKS
Hickory	Strong smoke flavor	Beef and pork
Mesquite	Strong smoke flavor	Beef and seafood
Apple	Mild, dense fruit flavor, sweet smoke and most common of fruitwoods	Pork, chicken, sides and desserts
Cherry	Subtly sweet fruity flavor, provides great color	Pork, chicken, seafood and desserts
Oak	Medium to heavy smoke flavor, slightly nutty	Beef
Alder	Light smoke flavor, mild wood	Seafood, vegetables and baked items
Pecan	Medium smoke flavor, sweet and mild flavor	Poultry, pork, vegetables and desserts
Maple	Mild, sweet flavor	Poultry, seafood and vegetables

FROM *the* SMOKER

THERE IS A CERTAIN LEVEL OF PATIENCE that is required to cook a great meal in the smoker, and for those with a Traeger that is now an everyday option. Today, smoking, in terms of barbecue, is a method of slow roasting with the addition of smoke flavor in an enclosed form of cooking equipment. Natural hardwood smoke adds nitrates to meats and causes a chemical reaction in them, most noticeably in the form of a smoke ring. With literally the push of a button, a Traeger's easy ability to fire up eliminates the need to spend time managing a fire. In addition, just by changing the pellets in your hopper you can change the wood flavor profile of your cook.

BACON-WRAPPED MEATBALLS
(aka Moink Balls)

COOK TIME: 45–55 MINUTES · YIELD: 24 MEATBALLS

Make these at your next BBQ and I assure you they will go faster than any appetizer you put out. These little bites of soft, crunchy, salty goodness are effortless to make and a delicious start to any get-together. We like to give them a nice brush of our BBQ sauce to add a sweet heat to finish them off. If you have a favorite meatball recipe, feel free to use that in lieu of the frozen ones listed in this recipe. Just be sure to make them each about ½ ounce (14 g).

12 slices bacon

24 (½-oz [14-g]) frozen meatballs, thawed

¼ cup (36 g) dry rub (see pages 133–141)

1 cup (240 ml) BBQ sauce (see pages 142–150)

Prepare your Traeger by turning it to the SMOKE setting. Wait about 5 minutes for it to produce smoke, then set the Traeger to run at 275°F (135°C).

Slice the bacon in half lengthwise to make 24 pieces. Wrap each meatball in a slice of the bacon and secure with a toothpick. After all 24 meatballs are wrapped, sprinkle the dry rub evenly on the meatballs to coat. Place the meatballs directly on the smoker grate and cook about 40 minutes or until they are about 155°F (70°C). Brush the meatballs with the BBQ sauce and smoke another 10 to 15 minutes, until the internal temperature reaches 165°F (75°C).

Note: For crispier bacon, increase the temperature of your smoker to 375°F (190°C) during the last 15 minutes of your cook.

BACON-WRAPPED STUFFED JALAPEÑOS

COOK TIME: 60 MINUTES · YIELD: 24 JALAPEÑO POPPERS

This recipe is great in that even though it's a jalapeño, the heat factor is drastically cut down by the use of cream cheese, which makes for more of a poblano rating on the Scoville scale. Of course if heat is what you're looking for, be sure to leave in some of the ribs and seeds of the jalapeño to kick it up a notch. This recipe has it all: a bit of heat from the pepper and sweetness from the cream cheese and rub—and saltiness from the bacon just brings it all together. When preparing the jalapeños, I'll share a little tip that was definitely learned by experience: Wear disposable gloves!

12 jalapeños, 3 to 4 inches (8 to 10 cm) in size

1 (8-oz [227-g]) package cream cheese, softened

1 cup (115 g) shredded cheese (cheddar, Monterey Jack, pepper Jack or taco blend)

¼ cup (36 g) sugar-forward rub (such as Meat Church Honey Hog BBQ Rub)

12 slices bacon

Prepare your Traeger by turning it to the SMOKE setting. Wait about 5 minutes for it to produce smoke, then set the Traeger to run at 275°F (135°C).

Slice the tops off the jalapeños as close to the stem as possible. Slice the jalapeño vertically and using your (gloved) finger or a small spoon, scoop out all the ribs and seeds and discard them.

In a bowl, mix the cream cheese, shredded cheese and rub until combined.

Slice the bacon in half vertically to make 24 pieces.

Spoon (or pipe, using a food storage bag) the cheese mixture into the jalapeños, then wrap each with a piece of bacon. Place the jalapeños on a sheet tray and put the tray on the smoker for 30 minutes.

Increase the temperature of the smoker to 375°F (190°C) and smoke another 30 minutes to crisp the bacon.

CITRUSY BRINED CORNISH HENS

COOK TIME: 1 HOUR 45 MINUTES · YIELD: 4 SERVINGS

The citrus in this dish lightens up the gamey flavor found in Cornish hens. Due to the small nature of these birds, they tend to have a lower fat content. Brining ensures they won't get dry during the cooking process. These are great around the holidays when you have guests coming over, as the presentation of Cornish hens is almost as appealing as the taste. Serve these with the Balsamic-Glazed Roasted Brussels Sprouts with Bacon (page 93).

4 cups (1 L) vegetable broth

4 cups (1 L) cold water

1 tbsp (10 g) whole black peppercorns

¼ cup (55 g) brown sugar

1 cup (250 g) kosher salt

4 Cornish game hens

2 lemons

2 medium oranges

2 tbsp (24 g) ground coriander

1 tsp ginger

1 tsp cumin

¼ cup (60 ml) olive oil

Salt and pepper to taste

To make the brine, bring the vegetable broth, water, black peppercorns, sugar and salt to a boil in a large pot, stirring until the salt is dissolved. Remove the brine from the heat and set aside to cool. When the brine is cool, place the Cornish hens in the brine and refrigerate for 2 to 3 hours. Do not overbrine or the hens will get too salty.

Prepare your Traeger by turning it to the SMOKE setting. Wait about 5 minutes for it to produce smoke, then set the Traeger to run at 350°F (175°C).

Remove the hens from the brine, and pat dry. Discard the brine.

Cut the lemons and oranges into quarters and place in a microwave-safe bowl and sprinkle with the coriander, ginger and cumin. Microwave on high for 2 minutes. Using a spoon or tongs, stuff the mixture into the cavities of the Cornish hens. Brush each hen with the olive oil and sprinkle with salt and pepper. Place the stuffed hens into a disposable aluminum half-size tray, breast sides up.

Roast the hens for about 1 hour and 45 minutes or until an instant-read thermometer inserted into the thickest part of the thigh near the bone reads 180°F (82°C).

For crispier skin, increase the heat to 400°F (205°C) for the last 15 minutes of cooking.

Rest the hens for 10 minutes before serving. Resting the meat before serving helps to prevent the juices from running out when sliced.

TURKEY BREAST STUFFED
with Gruyère Cheese and Spinach
COOK TIME: 1 HOUR · YIELD: 8 SERVINGS

A boneless turkey breast stuffed with savory flavors is perfect for Sunday dinner or special enough for a small holiday dinner. If you buy a boneless half turkey breast, it will probably be skinless. You may find bone-in, skin-on breast as well; ask your butcher to bone it for you or bone it yourself.

1 (3- to 4-lb [1.4- to 1.8-kg]) whole turkey breast (boneless)

1 cup (30 g) baby spinach, coarsely chopped

½ cup (54 g) shredded Gruyère cheese

¼ cup (45 g) All-Around BBQ Rub (page 133)

Prepare your Traeger by turning it to the SMOKE setting. Wait about 5 minutes for it to produce smoke, then set the Traeger to run at 325°F (165°C).

Using a sharp knife, slice the turkey breast horizontally, making sure not to slice all the way through it. Lay it open and spread the spinach and cheese evenly onto the turkey breast, pressing lightly to ensure the filling adheres. Carefully roll the turkey breast tightly and tie with butcher's twine at intervals of about 1½ inches (4 cm; or a thumb's width). Gently season the outside of the turkey breast with the BBQ rub and place the prepared breast directly on the grill grate for 60 minutes.

Your turkey breast will be done when the internal temperature reaches 165°F (75°C). When the temperature is reached, remove the turkey breast from the grill and let it rest for 15 minutes. Then, slice and serve immediately.

Note: We love smoking with poultry; however, it is a sponge for smoke. We suggest going with a lighter, fruitier wood to smoke with, like cherry or apple, so you do not overpower your guests' taste buds.

SMOKED PULLED TURKEY BREAST

COOK TIME: 3½–4½ HOURS • YIELD: 8 SERVINGS

Pulled pork is one of those legendary recipes you probably made shortly after you purchased your Traeger. The long cook results in a wonderfully tender, smoked piece of meat that is perfect for sandwiches. However, you can smoke more than just pork. I love making pulled chicken and turkey on my Traeger. Just like the pork version, you will need to find meat with some fat in it—using a bone-in turkey breast has provided me with some great results.

1 (3- to 4-lb [1.4- to 1.8-kg]) whole turkey breast (with bone)

¼ cup (36 g) poultry dry rub (with salt)

1 cup (227 g) unsalted butter

1 package potato bun sliders (optional)

1 cup (240 ml) BBQ sauce, for serving (see pages 142–150)

Prepare your Traeger by turning it to the SMOKE setting. Wait about 5 minutes for it to produce smoke, then set the Traeger to run at 250°F (120°C).

Remove the skin from the turkey breast and discard it. Rub the turkey breast liberally with your favorite poultry rub on all sides. Place the turkey breast on a disposable aluminum half-size tray and cover the tray with foil. Smoke for about 2½ hours, until lightly browned.

Remove the breast from the smoker and prepare two large sheets of heavy-duty aluminum foil (about double the size of the breast). Place the butter on top of the turkey breast and wrap tightly with both sheets of foil, one at a time, making sure the breast is completely covered.

Return the breast to the smoker for another 1 to 2 hours, or until an instant-read thermometer inserted into the center of the breast reads 160°F (70°C). Allow the turkey to cool slightly, then pull the meat apart using your hands or two forks.

Place the turkey on the sliders and top with your favorite BBQ sauce.

BEER CAN CHICKEN

COOK TIME: 3 HOURS · YIELD: 4–6 SERVINGS

Beer can chicken is just one of the fun things that people love to make in the Traeger. While the science seems to indicate that the beer isn't all that essential to the cooking process, it's entertaining to use and as you know, presentation plays a big part in a meal.

I'm a big fan of brining poultry (see page 55). During brining some of the salt and water is drawn into the meat and you can really taste the difference in the finished product. The typical rule of thumb is to brine a whole chicken 1 hour for every pound (454 g).

1 (12-oz [355-ml]) can of your favorite beer

1 (4-lb [1.8-kg]) whole chicken

½ cup (115 g) mayonnaise

⅓ cup (60 g) your favorite BBQ rub (see pages 133–141)

Open the can of beer and discard half. (But remember, smoking a chicken is hard work and you need to stay hydrated—just saying!)

Lower the cavity of the chicken over the top of the can with the legs supporting some of the weight. Arrange the chicken in a half-size disposable aluminum pan so that the can is holding up the chicken with legs pointed downward. We prefer to cook in an aluminum pan for two reasons. One is that it will better support the weight of the chicken. Second, it will catch and retain the drippings, which keeps the smoker clean and lets the fire burn pure.

In a small bowl, combine the mayonnaise and rub and mix thoroughly. Pat the chicken dry and then, using your hands, rub the mixture all over the bird. Don't be bashful—more is better here.

Prepare your Traeger by turning it to the SMOKE setting. Wait about 5 minutes for it to produce smoke, then set the Traeger to run at 225°F (110°C).

Place your beer can chicken in the pan on the Traeger and cook for 1 hour. After 1 hour, increase the temperature to 300°F (150°C) and cook for 2 hours, or until the internal temperature of the meat in the breast reaches 165°F (75°C). I recommend cooking this way as the lower heat produces more smoke so cooking in two stages allows you to get a great smoke flavor and a perfectly cooked chicken.

Remove the pan from the Traeger, tent with some foil and let the chicken rest for 15 minutes before slicing.

*See photo on page 12.

Note: We prefer to use pecan or apple wood for a whole chicken.

SAUSAGE & PEPPER FATTY

COOK TIME: 2 HOURS · YIELD: 6 SERVINGS

A sausage fatty is a roll of delicious ingredients wrapped up in a neat little package. It's an explosion of flavor in every bite. A fatty is extremely versatile in that it can be eaten as an appetizer, breakfast, lunch or dinner. In addition to this Sausage & Pepper Fatty, in this book we give you two more stuffing ideas—see the Blueberry Sausage Fatty on page 29 and the Pizza Fatty on page 101—but feel free to get as creative as you like with fillings.

With a flavor similar to the classic Italian-American sausage and pepper sandwich, this recipe is sure to be a crowd-pleaser for even the pickiest guests. This recipe takes old flavors and puts a new twist on them with the addition of bacon and BBQ sauce. We like to prepare this for lunch but really, you can eat it any time.

In this dish we also use a bacon weave, which adds flavor and structure to the dish. By wrapping bacon around the meat you will preserve the shape of the fatty. As the meat cooks, the fat and flavor from the bacon will seep into the meat, creating a juicy, salty and savory flavor.

1 lb (454 g) bacon

2 to 3 tbsp (18 to 27 g) pork rub

1 tbsp (15 ml) olive oil

1 medium onion (white, yellow, Spanish or sweet), peeled and sliced into ¼-inch (6-mm) strips

1 medium green pepper, stemmed, seeded and cut into ¼-inch (6-mm) strips

1 medium red pepper, stemmed, seeded and cut into ¼-inch (6-mm) strips

½ tsp salt

½ tsp black pepper

2 lb (908 g) ground sausage (your choice of hot, sweet or breakfast; without casing)

¼ cup (20 g) grated Parmesan cheese

Your favorite BBQ sauce (see pages 142–150), for serving

To create a bacon weave, lay eight slices of bacon vertically very close together on plastic wrap. The bacon slices should all be facing the same direction (fat side facing one way, meat side facing the other). Working with one strip at a time, arrange eight additional strips perpendicular to the first ones, weaving the strips over and under to form a lattice. Make sure your weave is as tight as possible when finished.

Sprinkle approximately 2 tablespoons (18 g) of the rub on the weave, adding more as necessary. You want your bacon weave to be well coated but not overly dredged. You should have a nice even covering of rub on the weave.

(Continued)

Sausage & Pepper Fatty (Continued)

Heat the oil in a large skillet over medium-high heat. Add the onion, peppers, salt and pepper, and cook about 5 minutes, or until soft. Allow the mixture to cool, then strain off excess water using a colander.

Layer the sausage directly on top of the bacon weave, patting down gently and keeping the same thickness throughout the layer (so it will cook evenly). Next, spoon the pepper mixture evenly on top of the sausage and sprinkle with Parmesan cheese. Carefully separate the front edge of the sausage layer from the bacon weave and begin rolling into a log. You want to include all layers except the bacon weave. Try to seal any holes and pinch off the ends. The sausage should now be in the shape of a log. Next, roll the sausage forward, wrapping it in the bacon weave. The bacon seam should be underneath the roll when you are done. Sprinkle more rub on the outside of the roll.

Meanwhile, prepare your Traeger by turning it to the SMOKE setting. Wait about 5 minutes for it to produce smoke, then set the Traeger to run at 250°F (120°C).

Place the sausage roll directly on the smoker grates and close the lid. Allow the roll to cook for about 2 hours, or until an instant-read thermometer inserted into the center of the roll reads 165°F (75°C).

Remove the roll from the smoker and allow it to cool for 5 minutes. Using a sharp knife, slice the roll into ½-inch (13-mm)-thick pieces. Drizzle with BBQ sauce before serving.

Note: Alternatively, you can place a bacon weave on top of a dish such as a quiche, which creates a beautiful presentation with a kicked-up flavor profile.

BLUEBERRY SAUSAGE FATTY

COOK TIME: 2 HOURS · YIELD: 6 SERVINGS

This recipe is the ultimate weekend breakfast treat: sweet, salty and savory. Competition cooking means long nights and early mornings, and this was something I started making to fill that time. Eventually friends and family convinced me to enter it in the Northeast Barbecue Society (NEBS) grilling competition. This fatty has won numerous awards, but more important, it puts a smile on everyone's face when they see it coming off the smoker. I like to serve it with a little drizzle of maple syrup on sliced pound cake that I toast right on the smoker. I recommend making the sausage roll the night before you plan to serve it, and turning on the smoker the first thing in the morning.

1 lb (454 g) bacon

1 (16-oz [454-g]) roll ground breakfast sausage (such as Jimmy Dean)

2 tbsp (18 g) pork rub

4 large store-bought blueberry muffins, preferably with sugar topping

6 slices pound cake, for serving (optional)

½ cup (120 ml) pure maple syrup, for serving

Create a bacon weave on plastic wrap (see page 25). Make sure your weave is as tight as possible when finished.

Layer the sausage directly on top of the bacon weave, patting down gently and keeping the same thickness throughout the layer (so it will cook evenly). Sprinkle the rub evenly over the sausage to coat. Next, using only the tops of the muffins, crumble the blueberry muffins with your hands onto the sausage. Make sure to cover the sausage with the muffins as evenly as possible.

Carefully separate the front edge of the sausage layer from the bacon weave and begin rolling into a log. You want to include all layers except the bacon weave. Try to seal any holes and pinch off the ends. The sausage should now be in the shape of a log. Next, roll the sausage forward, wrapping it in the bacon weave. The bacon seam should be underneath the roll when you are done.

Meanwhile, prepare your Traeger by turning it to the SMOKE setting. Wait about 5 minutes for it to produce smoke, then set the Traeger to run at 250°F (120°C).

Place your sausage roll directly on the smoker grates and close the lid. Allow the roll to cook for about 2 hours, or until an instant-read thermometer inserted into the center of the roll reads 165°F (75°C). Remove the roll from the smoker and allow it to cool for 5 minutes.

If serving this dish on pound cake, slice the cake into ¾-inch (2-cm) slices and put directly on the smoker grate with the lid open, turning once to toast both sides. Using a sharp knife, slice the roll into ½-inch (13-mm)-thick pieces. Drizzle with maple syrup before serving.

MAPLE-BOURBON PORK BELLY

COOK TIME: 5 HOURS · YIELD: 10–12 SERVINGS

Pork belly is pretty self-explanatory as it comes from the belly of the pig and is a fatty piece of boneless meat. The high fat content makes this piece of meat perfect for smoking using the low and slow method as the fat will render and meat will become bite tender. Pork belly when cured is most commonly know as bacon; however, for this recipe you'll want to purchase the uncured, thicker kind. Found in the pork section at the grocery store, or from your local butcher, it's usually about 1½ to 2 inches (4 to 5 cm) thick. This recipe calls for the pork to brine for three days so plan accordingly.

3 lb (1.4 kg) pork belly

1 tbsp (6 g) mustard powder

1 tsp cumin

¾ tsp freshly ground black pepper

1½ tbsp (27 g) kosher salt

¼ cup (60 ml) maple syrup

2 tbsp (30 ml) honey bourbon (such as Jack Honey)

Rinse and dry the pork belly. Remove the hard outer skin if present, cutting close to the edge of the fat to leave as much fat on the meat as possible.

Combine the mustard powder, cumin, black pepper and salt in a small bowl. Rub half of the mixture on the pork belly on all sides.

In a plastic resealable freezer bag, combine the maple syrup, bourbon and the remainder of the dry spice mixture. Place the pork belly in the plastic bag and massage to coat. Seal the bag, making sure to squeeze out excess air. Place the bag in the refrigerator; turn the bag over occasionally to ensure all ingredients coat the meat evenly. Refrigerate for at least 24 hours and up to 3 days.

When ready to cook, prepare your Traeger by turning it to the SMOKE setting. Wait about 5 minutes for it to produce smoke, then set the Traeger to run at 225°F (110°C).

Remove the pork belly from the brine and put it in a disposable aluminum pan, fat-side up. When the grill has reached the correct temperature, place the pan inside the smoker directly on the grates and close the door. Let the pork belly cook about 5 hours, or until the internal temperature reaches 174°F (79°C).

Remove the pork belly from the smoker and allow it to cool for about 5 minutes. Slice or cube and enjoy!

STICKY PORK TENDERLOIN

COOK TIME: 2½–3 HOURS · YIELD: 4 SERVINGS

The only similarity between a pork tenderloin like the one used in this recipe and a pork loin is the loin in the name. They look completely different: a tenderloin is much smaller at about 12 inches (30 cm) long and 3 inches (8 cm) wide and in the shape of a cylinder. A pork loin is wider and thicker and has more fat on it. Because of the lean nature of a pork tenderloin, we use a lower temperature to get a nice smoky flavor into the meat without drying it out.

2-inch (5-cm) piece fresh ginger

4 large cloves garlic

¾ cup (180 ml) soy sauce

½ cup (120 ml) honey

1 tbsp (15 ml) rice wine or white vinegar

1 tbsp (15 ml) olive oil

½ tsp black pepper

½ tsp ground chile

2 tbsp (15 g) cornstarch

1½ lb (680 g) pork tenderloin, silver skin removed if attached

Peel the ginger (I like to use the back of the spoon to get the skin off) and chop it coarsely. Lay the ginger on a cutting board and smash the ginger to release its aromas and flavors by taking the back of a chef knife and pressing it firmly onto the ginger. Do the same for the four cloves of garlic.

In a small pot over medium heat, add the soy sauce, honey, garlic, ginger, vinegar, olive oil, black pepper and ground chile. Stir until simmering, then add the cornstarch, stirring constantly. Remove from the heat when the mixture starts to boil. The sauce should be smooth and thicker than when you started.

Meanwhile, prepare your Traeger to run at 225°F (110°C).

Place the tenderloin in a disposable aluminum tray and pour the sauce over the tenderloin. Put the tray in the smoker and cook for 2½ to 3 hours or until the internal temperature reaches 145°F (62°C). Let the tenderloin rest for 5 minutes before slicing.

SMOKED MEATLOAF

COOK TIME: 2½ HOURS · YIELD: 6 SERVINGS

Meatloaf is something most all of us grew up eating for dinner during the week. It's easy to make, hearty and just about foolproof. I always like to put my take on nostalgic recipes and make them new and fresh. This recipe uses the classic mix of three different types of ground meat, but I add in some sharp cheddar for a nice bite and BBQ sauce in place of the traditional ketchup or tomato sauce. Add in the smoky flavor and tenderness you get from using the Traeger and you'll have a new weeknight staple.

¾ cup (180 ml) BBQ sauce (see pages 142–150), divided

¾ cup (120 g) diced yellow onion

2 cloves garlic, chopped

2 lb (908 g) ground meatloaf mix (pork, beef and veal)

1 cup (115 g) shredded sharp cheddar cheese

1 egg, beaten

1 tbsp (15 ml) Worcestershire sauce

1 tsp kosher salt

1 tsp ground black pepper

½ cup (35 g) seasoned bread crumbs

In a medium bowl, combine ¼ cup (60 ml) of the BBQ sauce with the onion, garlic, meatloaf mix, cheese, egg, Worcestershire sauce, salt, pepper and bread crumbs. Using your hands, work the mixture just until all the ingredients are combined. Shape the meat mixture into a football-sized loaf. Place the meatloaf in the refrigerator to firm up the shape while your Traeger is preheating.

Prepare your Traeger by turning it to the SMOKE setting. Wait about 5 minutes for it to produce smoke, then set the Traeger to run at 225°F (110°C).

Place the meatloaf directly on the smoker grate and close the lid. After 1 hour and 30 minutes, brush with the remaining ½ cup (120 ml) of BBQ sauce and close the lid to cook for about another hour or until the internal temperature of the meatloaf reaches 160°F (70°C).

SMOKED FRENCH DIP AU JUS

COOK TIME: 1 HOUR 20 MINUTES · YIELD: 6 SERVINGS

This savory and smoky sandwich will leave your hands covered in delicious meat drippings and will be well worth the mess. The natural juices from the meat and onions will commingle during the smoking process and leave you with a flavorful dipping sauce when the cook is over. We stop the cooking process at 130°F (55°C) because you don't want to overcook this roast, or it will become tough and dry.

4 lb (1.8 kg) round-eye roast

2 tbsp (30 g) yellow mustard

2 tbsp (18 g) beef rub

1 medium onion, thinly sliced

Salt and pepper to taste

2 cups (480 ml) water

4 oz (120 ml) au jus base (such as Johnny's, usually in the gravy aisle of the supermarket)

6 Portuguese rolls or 3 medium baguettes

12 slices provolone cheese

Prepare your Traeger by turning it to the SMOKE setting. Wait about 5 minutes for it to produce smoke, then set the Traeger to run at 250°F (120°C).

Rub all sides of the roast with the mustard and sprinkle with the beef rub to coat. Place the sliced onion in a disposable aluminum half-tray and season with salt and pepper. Place the roast on a baking rack. Place the rack in the aluminum pan over the onions, then place the pan in the preheated Traeger and close the lid.

Allow the onions to cook for 20 minutes, then pour in the water and au jus base. Close the smoker lid. Cook for about 1 hour more, turning the roast over once, halfway through the cook. Remove the roast from the smoker when the internal temperature reads 120°F (50°C) for rare, or 130°F (55°C) for medium rare.

Let the roast rest for 30 minutes. Slice the roast as thinly as possible and place the sliced pieces in the pan with the au jus and onion. Cut the Portuguese rolls in half lengthwise (if not presliced) or slice your baguettes in half in the middle to make six pieces, then slice each lengthwise. Layer each roll with slices of the meat and two pieces of provolone. Place the sandwich directly on the smoker grates and close the lid. Heat just until the cheese is melted. Serve with a side of the au jus for dipping.

CHEESY SMOKED GRITS

COOK TIME: 1 HOUR · YIELD: 6 SERVINGS

Grits are something I fell in love with while visiting relatives down South. It was a staple on the breakfast table and the norm for everyone except me. I couldn't get enough of them and soon started experimenting with different ingredients, but always coming back to the traditional flavors. This recipe includes my favorite grits ingredients: butter and cheese. The smoky flavor from the Traeger exemplifies the smoky cheese flavor and everything melds together seamlessly.

Please note you will need a cast-iron skillet for this recipe.

5 cups (1.2 L) water

1½ tsp (9 g) salt

½ tsp black pepper

½ tsp garlic powder

1½ cups (235 g) quick (not instant) grits

12 tbsp (170 g) unsalted butter

⅓ cup (80 ml) heavy cream

12 oz (340 g) shredded smoked cheddar

Hot sauce of choice, optional, for serving

Prepare your Traeger by turning it to the SMOKE setting. Wait about 5 minutes for it to produce smoke, then set the Traeger to run at 350°F (175°C).

In a large saucepan, boil the water, salt, pepper and garlic powder. Add the grits and reduce the heat to simmer, stirring occasionally until thickened, about 7 minutes. Remove the pot from the heat and add the butter, heavy cream and smoked cheddar. Mix until combined. Pour the grits into a 10-inch (25-cm) cast-iron skillet and place directly on the Traeger grates and close the lid for 45 minutes. The grits should be bubbly and slightly browned on top. Let them cool slightly and serve in bowls with hot sauce if desired.

APPLE PIE BAKED BEANS

COOK TIME: 1½ HOURS · YIELD: 12 SERVINGS

Baked beans are a perfect complement to the barbecue main dish. This is a quick and easy modification of a timeless classic. We love how the apple pie filling makes this a sweet and savory dish.

1 (20-oz [565-g]) can apple pie filling

1 (55-oz [1.6-kg]) can Bush's Original Baked Beans

½ cup (120 ml) BBQ sauce of your choice (see pages 142–150)

2 tbsp (18 g) rub of your choice (see pages 133–141)

Prepare your Traeger by turning it to the SMOKE setting. Wait about 5 minutes for it to produce smoke, then set the Traeger to run at 325°F (165°C).

Place the apple pie filling in a blender to lightly chop the large apple chunks. You still want to have small pieces of apple throughout the mixture so don't go crazy here with blending.

In a disposable aluminum half-size tray, combine the beans, chopped apple pie filling, BBQ sauce and rub.

Place the tray in your Traeger and close the lid for 1½ hours. Remove the beans from the smoker and serve hot.

COFFEE-RUBBED TRI-TIP STEAK

COOK TIME: 75 MINUTES · YIELD: 4 SERVINGS

Smoked tri-tip is one of my favorite cuts of beef that I cook on the smoker. It is tender, delicious and doesn't take a long time to prepare. Tri-tip is customarily found on the West Coast and is starting to gain popularity on the East Coast. It has great marbling and will stay super moist during the cooking process. In this version, I used a rub that incorporates coffee as well as an ancho chile powder, which really make that delicious beef flavor pop. I think you're going to like this one a lot!

1 (2- to 3-lb [0.9- to 1.4-kg]) tri-tip roast

2 tbsp (16 g) ancho chile powder

2 tbsp (11 g) finely ground coffee beans

5 tsp (23 g) dark brown sugar

1 tbsp (8 g) hot smoked Spanish paprika

1½ tsp (2 g) dried oregano

1½ tsp (3 g) freshly ground black pepper

1½ tsp (6 g) ground coriander

1½ tsp (3 g) mustard powder

1 tsp chile de árbol powder or ¾ tsp finely ground red pepper flakes

1 tsp ground ginger

1 tbsp (18 g) kosher salt, plus more as needed

A tri-tip roast will usually have a fat cap on one side and silver skin on the other. If the butcher has not already trimmed these, remove them with a knife.

Mix the ancho chile powder, ground coffee, brown sugar, paprika, oregano, pepper, coriander, mustard powder, chile de árbol powder, ginger and the salt in a small bowl. Season both sides of the roast evenly with the spice rub (save any extra rub for your next cook). Place the roast on a wire rack set inside a rimmed baking sheet and chill uncovered for 3 to 6 hours.

Let the roast sit for 1 hour to come to room temperature, which will help it cook quickly and more evenly.

Prepare your Traeger by turning it to the SMOKE setting (see Note). Wait about 5 minutes for it to produce smoke, then set the Traeger to run at 275°F (135°C).

Place the baking sheet with the roast on your Traeger and cook for 1 hour or until the internal temperature reaches 130°F (55°F). Remove the roast from the Traeger and turn it up to the highest setting. When your Traeger is up to temperature on its highest setting, remove the roast from the pan and place it directly on the grill for 3 minutes per side to achieve a nice sear. The internal temperature will be approximately 140°F (60°F). Let the roast rest for 15 minutes before slicing. You will want to slice the tri-tip across the grain in ¼-inch (6-mm)-thick slices.

Note: While beef typically gets smoked with hickory, mesquite or oak, we prefer a fruitwood for our tri-tip. Cherry, apple and pecan are all favorites; experiment and see what you like the best!

SMOKED ARMADILLO "EGGS"

COOK TIME: 1½ HOURS · YIELD: 20 PIECES

One of my all-time favorite appetizers is smoked armadillo "eggs." Perfect for serving while you're waiting on the brisket or pork shoulder to be done, guests will go crazy when they bite into one and realize the inside is hot and creamy and oozing goodness with every bite.

8 oz (227 g) cream cheese

1 cup (115 g) shredded cheddar cheese

¼ cup (36 g) BBQ rub (see pages 133–141), divided

10 jalapeños

1 lb (454 g) ground breakfast sausage

Combine the cream cheese and cheddar cheese in a bowl. Stir in 1 tablespoon (9 g) of the BBQ rub.

Cut the stem off the jalapeños and slice them in half lengthwise, then remove the seeds and ribs.

Stuff about a teaspoon of the cream cheese mixture in the hollow of each pepper.

Press the sausage out onto a nonstick surface to make one flat, even layer. Lay one of the stuffed jalapeños onto the sausage and cut a piece of the sausage big enough to wrap around the jalapeño. Wrap the sausage around the jalapeño, forming it into an egg shape.

Spread the remainder of the rub onto a plate or flat surface and roll the sausage egg in the rub, making sure all sides are well coated.

Meanwhile, prepare your Traeger by turning it to the SMOKE setting (see Note). Wait about 5 minutes for it to produce smoke, then set the Traeger to run at 225°F (110°C).

Place the armadillo eggs directly on the grate. After 1½ hours they should have an internal temperature of 165°F (75°C).

Note: We really like the color and taste of cherry pellets for our armadillo eggs; however, they also go great with pecan, apple and hickory.

TEXAS-STYLE BEEF BRISKET

COOK TIME: 11–14 HOURS • YIELD: 15–20 PIECES

Mention the word *brisket* to nearly anyone and they will probably have an opinion about everything from where the best brisket is made to what part is their favorite. One thing that all pitmasters can agree on is that if you are going to make a brisket, you must use a full packer, which means a whole beef brisket.

1 (12- to 15-lb [5.4- to 6.8-kg]) whole packer brisket

1 cup (225 g) yellow mustard

½ cup (125 g) kosher salt

½ cup (55 g) ground black pepper, café grind (see page 153)

Trim the fat cap off the top of the brisket and remove all silver skin. We also like to trim the sides of the brisket to square it up so there will be an even cook. Trim the bottom fat cap to about a ¼ inch (6 mm) thickness. This excess fat will provide moisture throughout your cook.

Rub the entire brisket with the yellow mustard. The mustard will act as a binder for the salt and pepper rub. It doesn't have to be perfect; the mustard will have no effect on your cook. In a small bowl, combine the salt and pepper and mix well. If you have an empty shaker bottle/dredge you could use that as well. When evenly mixed, apply an even layer of the salt-and-pepper mixture over the brisket. Make sure to turn the brisket over and apply the salt and pepper to the fat cap side as well.

Meanwhile, prepare your Traeger by turning it to the SMOKE setting. Wait about 5 minutes for it to produce smoke, then set the Traeger to run at 225°F (110°C).

Place the brisket directly on the grill grate, fat-side down, and cook for 8 hours. After 8 hours, take a temperature reading of the brisket once in the point area and once in the flat. If the temperature is not at 160°F (70°C), close the lid and monitor the temperature every 30 minutes. When the brisket registers to 160°F (70°C), double wrap it with foil or butcher paper. Place the wrapped brisket back on the grill grate and continue to cook for another 3 hours.

After 3 hours, test for doneness. While most assess doneness by a certain temperature, we like to go by feel. Using a toothpick or the end of your thermometer, you should be able to penetrate the brisket with little resistance. It should feel almost as though you are putting the toothpick or thermometer probe through a warm stick of butter. Ideally the internal temperature you should find for this level of tenderness is 205°F (96°C).

When done, remove the brisket from the grill; let the foil or butcher paper vent for 3 to 5 minutes to stop the cooking process. Then, close the wrapping and wrap the brisket in a towel and place it in an empty cooler to rest for at least an hour. When ready to serve, slice the brisket across the grain. Each slice should be roughly a ¼ inch (6 mm) thick. Pitmasters often think of this as being the thickness of a #2 pencil.

SMOKED CORNED BEEF BRISKET
(aka Pastrami)

COOK TIME: 4½–5 HOURS · YIELD: 8–10 SERVINGS

On St. Patty's Day you will find everyone and their mother making corned beef and cabbage. This great recipe is a variation of a timeless classic and something that will turn the heads of your guests. Pastrami is simply a corned beef brisket seasoned with spices and then smoked until tender.

3 to 4 lb (1.4 to 1.8 kg) corned beef brisket flat

8 oz (227 g) coarse or whole grain mustard

⅓ cup (48 g) your favorite BBQ rub (see pages 133–141)

Prepare your Traeger by turning it to the SMOKE setting (see Note). Wait about 5 minutes for it to produce smoke, then set the Traeger to run at 225°F (110°C).

Discard the seasoning packet that comes with the corned beef brisket. Making sure the fat cap side is down, apply a coat of mustard to the top and sides of the brisket. Next, apply a coat of BBQ rub onto the top and sides of the brisket. Making sure you keep the fat cap–side up, place the brisket into an aluminum pan. Place on the Traeger.

Allow the meat to cook for 2½ hours or until it reaches 140°F (60°F) in the thickest part. Then cover the aluminum pan with foil to allow the meat to braise for the remainder of the cook.

Allow the brisket to cook for an additional 2 to 2½ hours, until it has an internal temperature of 185°F (85°C). Remove the roast and let it rest for 30 minutes before carving. Make sure you remember to slice across the grain.

Note: For our pastrami, we enjoy using a blend of hickory and cherry wood pellets.

ST. LOUIS–STYLE PORK RIBS

COOK TIME: 4–4½ HOURS · YIELD: 8–10 SERVINGS

These sweet and spicy ribs are full of flavor. This is the same recipe and process that has resulted in numerous championship calls for our Handsome Devil team.

4 racks St. Louis–cut spareribs

1 cup (190 g) Rib Rub (page 137)

16 oz (480 ml) honey

2 cups (440 g) brown sugar

8 tbsp (112 g) butter

2½ cups (600 ml) Traditional BBQ Sauce (page 142), divided

Lay out the ribs with the meat side facing down. Apply the rub to the back side of the ribs, then let it set up for about 10 minutes. Flip the ribs over and apply the rub to the meat side, let the rub set on the ribs for about 15 minutes, then apply another coating of rub. Let sit for another 30 minutes.

Prepare your Traeger by turning it to the SMOKE setting. Wait about 5 minutes for it to produce smoke, then set the Traeger to run at 225°F (110°C).

Put the racks, meat-side up, directly on the grate and cook for 3 hours.

Lay out four sheets of heavy-duty foil, then apply 2 ounces (60 ml) of honey, ¼ cup (55 g) of brown sugar and 2 tablespoons (57 g) of butter to each sheet. Lay one rack of ribs, meat-side down, on each sheet. Apply another 2 ounces (60 ml) of honey, ¼ cup (55 g) of brown sugar and ½ cup (120 ml) of BBQ sauce to each rack, then wrap each rack tightly. You may want to double- wrap your ribs to keep the ribs from tearing through when putting them back on the BBQ.

Return the foil-wrapped ribs to the BBQ and cook for about 1 more hour, then check the ribs for doneness. To check if the ribs are done, look at the back side of the ribs. The meat will have shrunk from the bone about ¼ to ½ inch (6 to 13 mm) and the bones will have started to pop through on the back. If the ribs are done, remove the packets from the BBQ and open the foil to let them vent for about 10 minutes. This will stop them from cooking any further.

Take about ½ cup (120 ml) of juices from the foil and mix with ½ cup (120 ml) of the BBQ sauce. Brush the glaze over the ribs. Cut the ribs and serve.

FROM the GRILL

GRILLING IS DONE ALL OVER THE WORLD in various ways in various cultures, but all follow the same basic guideline of cooking over high direct heat for a relatively short amount of time. Grillmasters like to throw around the terms "direct heat" and "indirect heat" to impress guests. Direct heat is exactly what you think it is—when you place the food directly over the heat source. Grilling over indirect heat is a little more difficult to master than direct heat but once you have it down you're on the road to becoming a grillmaster. The basic concept is to cook your food slowly over heat that is close, but not directly under the food.

When it comes to grilling, heat is the name of the game. Because grilling takes less time than smoking, heat level and location of your food in relation to the heat source makes all the difference. The benefit of owning a Traeger is a clean, hot fire that burns at a true, consistent temperature.

JUICY BRINED CHICKEN BREAST

COOK TIME: 20 MINUTES · YIELD: 6 SERVINGS

This recipe is incredibly easy and versatile. After a long weekend of BBQ competitions and events where we indulge maybe a little too much, we like to lighten it up with a simple chicken that doesn't taste like "diet food." We make a big batch of this on Sunday to eat during the week for lunch and dinner. This chicken pairs well with salads; in wraps, quesadillas or tacos; or just on its own with a side of rice and veggies. The flavor is mild but satisfying, and the chicken is tasty and juicy.

Brine

½ cup (110 g) brown sugar

½ cup (125 g) kosher salt

1 qt (1 L) room-temperature water

2 tbsp (20 g) whole peppercorns

2 cloves garlic, crushed

6 thick chicken breasts, boneless and skinless

Rub

2 tsp (15 g) kosher salt

1 tsp ground black pepper

1 tsp garlic powder

1 tsp smoked paprika

½ tsp coriander

½ tsp cumin

2 tbsp (30 ml) olive oil

To make the brine, dissolve the brown sugar and salt in the water in a large pot. Add the peppercorns and crushed garlic. Add the chicken, making sure the chicken is completely submerged in brine mixture. Place the pot in the refrigerator for 2 hours. Make sure not to leave the chicken in the brine any longer than 2 hours—doing so can lead to an overly salty end product. Remove the chicken from the pot, rinse and pat dry.

Set your Traeger to HIGH and close the lid for 15 minutes to preheat.

While your Traeger is preheating, make the rub. Combine the salt, black pepper, garlic powder, paprika, coriander and cumin in a small bowl.

Coat the chicken lightly with the olive oil, making sure to cover all sides. Sprinkle the chicken liberally with rub on all sides. Place the chicken directly on the grates of the preheated Traeger and cook on each side 5 to 8 minutes or until the internal temperature reaches 165°F (75°C). Let rest for 10 minutes before serving.

GENERAL TSO'S CHICKEN WINGS

COOK TIME: 45–60 MINUTES · YIELD: 24 PIECES

The first wing competition I entered was with this General Tso's–inspired recipe. Just imagine your favorite sweet and spicy General Tso's sauce now covering crispy, sticky wings that are grilled and not baked. The balance of sweet and heat make it the kind of sauce you will want to put on everything.

The addition of baking powder in the rub will help crisp up your chicken skin. Baking powder is composed of an acid, which draws moisture to the surface of the chicken where it evaporates and cooks, accelerating the process so your chicken can get crispy.

Rub

2 tbsp (28 g) baking powder

1 tbsp (5 g) ground ginger

1 tsp salt

1 tsp onion powder

1 tsp garlic powder

½ tsp cayenne pepper

24 jumbo party wings
(about 3 lb [1.4 kg])

Sesame Ginger Sauce

⅓ cup (80 ml) soy sauce

⅓ cup (80 ml) sweet rice wine

⅓ cup (80 ml) water

1 tbsp (15 ml) sesame oil

2 tsp (10 ml) Sriracha

1 tbsp (5 g) ground ginger

2 cloves garlic, minced

1 tbsp (8 g) cornstarch

Salt and pepper to taste

3 tbsp (45 ml) water

½ cup (100 g) sugar

Preheat the Traeger to 375°F (190°C).

To make the rub, in a medium bowl, mix the baking powder, ground ginger, salt, onion powder, garlic powder and cayenne pepper together. Add half of the rub to a large resealable plastic bag. Add half of the wings and shake until coated evenly. Remove the wings from the bag and put them on a tray; make sure none of them are touching. Add the remaining rub and wings to the plastic bag and repeat the process.

Place the wings on the grill and watch closely so the wings do not burn. Flip the wings after 30 minutes and grill the other side until crispy, 15 to 30 minutes more.

To make the sesame ginger sauce, in a medium bowl, whisk together the soy sauce, sweet rice wine, water, sesame oil, Sriracha, ginger, garlic, cornstarch, salt and pepper. Set aside. Add the water and sugar to a medium skillet and boil over medium heat for 1 minute. Do not overcook. Add the soy sauce mixture and simmer until thickened, about 2 minutes. Remove the sauce from the heat and allow to cool slightly. Add the cooked chicken to a large bowl, then add the sauce. Toss until the wings are evenly coated.

STUFFED BELLY BURGER

COOK TIME: 6–10 MINUTES · YIELD: 4 BURGERS

As the name implies, this burger will leave you stuffed! Topped with slices of bacon and served on a Hawaiian roll, this is the ultimate in satisfying burgers. We like to stuff ours with cheddar, but feel free to use any cheese you like. To kick up the heat try a Monterey Jack, horseradish, or for the daring, habanero pepper cheese. We use the leftovers from our Maple-Bourbon Pork Belly (page 30; see Note) for this recipe, due to the time-consuming nature of smoking a pork belly.

2 lb (910 g) ground chuck (80/20 blend)

½ cup (72 g) BBQ rub (see pages 133–141), divided

8 oz (227 g) shredded sharp cheddar cheese

4 Hawaiian hamburger buns

1 recipe Maple-Bourbon Pork Belly (page 30)

¼ cup (60 ml) BBQ sauce (see pages 142–150)

Prepare your Traeger to run on HIGH.

In a medium bowl, add the ground chuck and ¼ cup (36 g) of the rub. Combine just until mixed, making sure not to overwork the meat. Overworking the meat will lead to a less tender burger.

Divide the meat into four equal-size balls (½ lb [227 g] each in size). If you have one, use a scale to make sure the balls are even. Using your thumb, make a 1-inch (3-cm)-deep well in the center of each burger. Put 2 ounces (57 g) of cheese in each hole, then close the burger over itself to form a ball again. After the burgers are stuffed, flatten them out slightly with your hands and sprinkle both sides of the burgers with the remaining rub.

Place the patties on the preheated grill and close the lid for 2 to 3 minutes. Flip the burgers and continue cooking for another 2 to 3 minutes for rare (120 to 125°F [50 to 52°C]), 4 to 5 minutes for medium rare (130 to 135°F [55 to 57°C]) and 6 to 7 minutes for medium (140 to 145°F [60 to 62°C]).

Allow the burgers to rest for 5 minutes to retain the juices before layering them on the buns and topping with equal amounts of the pork belly and BBQ sauce.

Note: If you're short on time, for each burger substitute two slices of grilled bacon sprinkled with a rub containing sugar (see pages 133–138) in place of the pork belly.

GRILLED HALIBUT
with Mango Salsa

COOK TIME: 10 MINUTES · YIELD: 4 SERVINGS

The flavor of the mango salsa and meatiness of the grilled halibut work together so well the only seasoning the fish will need is some Seafood Rub (page 141).

Mango Salsa

2 ripe Ataulfo mangos, peeled, pitted and diced

12 cherry or grape tomatoes, quartered

1 small red onion, diced

2 tbsp (30 ml) lime juice

2 tbsp (2 g) cilantro, chopped

1 tsp granulated sugar

½ tsp garlic powder

½ tsp kosher salt

¼ tsp ground black pepper

Halibut

1 lb (454 g) fresh halibut

2 tbsp (30 ml) olive oil

2 tbsp (18 g) Seafood Rub (page 141)

To make the salsa, in a medium bowl, combine the mangos, tomatoes, onion, lime juice, cilantro, sugar, garlic powder, salt and black pepper, mixing carefully so as not to crush the mangos and tomatoes. Taste and adjust seasonings (lime juice, salt, pepper) as desired. As the mixture sits, the flavors will meld together and the seasoning will be more prominent.

Set your Traeger to HIGH and close the lid for 15 minutes to preheat.

To make the halibut, rub the fish with olive oil, then sprinkle with the Seafood Rub. Allow the fish to rest for 5 minutes.

Oil the grill grates and place the fish directly on them and cook for about 5 minutes per side until the thickest part of the filet reads 140°F (60°C).

Remove the fish from the grill and top with the mango salsa.

AWARD-WINNING SHRIMP SCAMPI PIZZA

COOK TIME: 10–15 MINUTES · YIELD: 1 (14- TO 16-INCH [36- TO 41-CM]) PIZZA

The BBQ road team always get excited when they see we are competing in a Northeast Barbecue Society (NEBS) grilling competition because they know they will get to have some of this amazing pizza. The unique combination has won multiple awards throughout competitions in the Northeast and continues to wow all those who try it. The key is to start with a good-quality pizza dough and to use a well-heated pizza stone if you have one. Talk to your local pizza joint; they're usually more than willing to sell you raw pizza dough.

¾ cup (180 ml) extra virgin olive oil, divided

6 cloves garlic, chopped, divided

¼ cup (40 g) cornmeal or all-purpose flour

1 lb (454 g) fresh pizza dough

1 lb (454 g) black tiger 26/30–count shrimp, peeled and deveined

½ cup (40 g) freshly grated Parmesan

1½ cups (170 g) shredded mozzarella

1 cup (150 g) fresh cherry tomatoes, chopped

1 cup (42 g) fresh basil, chopped

Place a pizza stone in an unheated Traeger and set it to HIGH. Preheat for 30 minutes.

Mix ½ cup (120 ml) of the olive oil and 5 cloves of the chopped garlic until combined. Sprinkle cornmeal or flour onto a large cutting board or flat surface and work the dough into a 14- to 16-inch (36- to 41-cm) round shape.

Brush the olive oil mixture onto the pizza dough, covering as you would with a pizza sauce.

Slice the shrimp in half down the vein line and place them on the pizza, laying them flat in a pattern to cover most of the dough. Top the dough and shrimp with the Parmesan cheese. Finally, add the shredded mozzarella, being sure to cover the entire pie, as this is what will seal in the goodness.

Transport the pizza to the Traeger using the cutting board or a sheet pan turned upside down and place either on your preheated pizza stone or directly onto the grates. Close the smoker lid and allow to cook for 10 to 15 minutes, rotating halfway through the cooking process.

Meanwhile, mix the remaining ¼ cup (60 ml) of olive oil, 1 clove of garlic, chopped tomatoes and basil together in a small bowl. Drizzle the mixture over the pizza, slice and serve.

PIMENTO CHEESE
on *Grilled Baguette*

COOK TIME: 10 MINUTES · YIELD: 12 PIECES

Sometimes while your meat is marinating or you just want a quick appetizer that will impress your friends, you want to make something that is effortless but tasty. This southern snack was created after visiting Buxton Hall Barbecue restaurant on a summer BBQ tour vacation with my daughters and wife. We stumbled upon this cheese and were surprised at how satisfyingly delicious it was. You can add your own spices such as cayenne or jalapeños if you like spicy. Needless to say, when we returned home we decided we needed to re-create our own.

8 oz (227 g) cream cheese, softened

½ cup (58 g) grated sharp cheddar

½ cup (115 g) mayonnaise

½ tsp garlic powder

½ tsp onion powder

¼ tsp smoked paprika

1 (4-oz [114-g]) jar pimentos, drained

1 (12-inch [30-cm]) French baguette

Prepare your Traeger to run on HIGH.

Place the cream cheese in a food processor and beat until slightly whipped. If you do not have a food processor, beat the cream cheese with a hand mixer until whipped.

Add the sharp cheddar, mayonnaise, garlic powder, onion powder and smoked paprika and pulse or mix for 15 seconds more, just until the seasoning is combined and the cheddar is evenly incorporated. Add the drained pimentos and mix by hand until just combined.

Slice the baguette in half lengthwise and toast on the smoker grates until crispy. Spread the pimento cheese onto the bread and slice into 1-inch (3-cm) pieces.

MEXICAN STREET CORN

COOK TIME: 10 MINUTES · YIELD: 6 SERVINGS

I first had Mexican street corn—called elote—while vacationing in Mexico and was immediately intrigued by the unique flavors. It was unlike any corn I had had before and I couldn't figure out the flavors that were working so magically together. In my broken Spanish, I asked the gentleman making it for the ingredients and below is my interpretation of what he said.

½ cup (115 g) mayonnaise

½ cup (96 g) Mexican crema or sour cream

2 cloves garlic, minced

½ cup (60 g) crumbled queso fresco or cotija cheese

½ cup (8 g) chopped cilantro

1 tsp salt

½ tsp cayenne pepper

½ tsp chili powder

Canola or vegetable oil, for the grill

6 ears sweet corn, husks removed

1 large lime, cut in half

Prepare your Traeger to run on HIGH.

In a medium bowl, combine the mayonnaise, crema and garlic. Mix well and set aside. In a small bowl, mix the cheese and cilantro. Spread the cheese mixture on a flat surface such as a plate or sheet pan. In a small bowl, combine the salt, cayenne and chili powder.

Brush the Traeger grates with the oil and place the corn directly on the grates. Grill with the lid open about 10 minutes, turning often. The corn will be tender and slightly charred when done.

Remove the corn and quickly brush with the mayo mixture, then roll in the cheese mixture and sprinkle with the pepper mixture. Squeeze the lime over the corn and serve.

CHARLIE'S BLACKBERRY-GLAZED PORK TENDERLOIN

COOK TIME: 12–16 MINUTES · YIELD: 6 SERVINGS

This recipe comes from my friend, Charlie, in Atlanta. In the summer, it's all about the berries. The taste and smell of berries always reminds me of a day filled with sunshine. This pork tenderloin is the perfect summer supper main dish. The distinctive taste the blackberry creates makes the dish taste slightly sweet and light. Pair this with Chipotle Corn Whips (page 113) and Balsamic-Glazed Roasted Brussels Sprouts with Bacon (page 93) and you have yourself the perfect meal.

2 (1- to 1½-lb [454- to 680-g]) pork tenderloins

2 tbsp (30 ml) olive oil

2 tsp (15 g) kosher salt

1 tsp freshly ground black pepper

2 tsp (6 g) garlic powder

2 tsp (6 g) onion powder

Pinch of cayenne pepper

¾ cup (180 g) blackberry preserves (seedless)

Prepare your Traeger to run at 400°F (205°C).

Trim and clean the pork tenderloins of excess fat and silver skin. Coat each with the olive oil and season with the salt, black pepper, garlic powder, onion powder and cayenne pepper. Mix the blackberry preserves well with a fork, for easier spreading. Place the tenderloins on the preheated grate of the Traeger and generously brush all visible sides of the pork tenderloins with the blackberry preserves.

Leave the lid open and cook for 3 to 4 minutes, turn over and coat the other side with blackberry preserves. Turn over and brush on preserves twice more, cooking for 3 to 4 minutes each time, until an internal temperature of 145°F (62°C) is reached. Remove the tenderloins from the grill and allow the meat to rest for at least 10 minutes before slicing.

PROSCIUTTO & FRESH MOZZARELLA PIZZA

COOK TIME: 10–15 MINUTES · YIELD: 6 SERVINGS

As a New Yorker, I eat my fair share of pizza, from basic to gourmet. This combination of salty and savory is one of my favorites. Making it on the Traeger improves the flavor profile by infusing a subtle smokiness. The prosciutto crisps up nicely and the fresh mozzarella melts beautifully. Drizzling balsamic at the end cuts through the saltiness of the cheese and prosciutto.

¼ cup (40 g) cornmeal or all-purpose flour

1 lb (454 g) fresh pizza dough

8 oz (227 g) fresh mozzarella

4 medium plum tomatoes, sliced into ¼-inch (6-mm) slices

1 tsp Italian seasoning (salt-free)

2 tbsp (30 ml) olive oil

3 oz (85 g) prosciutto di Parma

Balsamic glaze, for drizzling

Place a pizza stone in an unheated Traeger and prepare to run on HIGH. Preheat for 30 minutes.

Sprinkle cornmeal or flour onto a large cutting board or flat surface and work the dough into a 14- to 16-inch (36- to 41-cm) round shape.

Slice the mozzarella into ½-inch (13-mm) slices and place on a paper towel to absorb extra moisture.

Top the pizza with the sliced tomatoes and fresh mozzarella and sprinkle with the Italian seasoning. Drizzle the pizza with the olive oil. Shred the prosciutto and place on the pizza.

Transport the pizza to the Traeger using the cutting board or a sheet pan turned upside down and place either on your preheated pizza stone or directly onto the grates of the grill. Close the smoker lid and allow the pizza to cook for 10 to 15 minutes, rotating halfway through the cooking process.

Remove the pizza from the smoker and drizzle lightly with balsamic glaze. Slice and serve.

LEMON-GARLIC SALMON

COOK TIME: 60 MINUTES · YIELD: 6-8 SERVINGS

I love seafood on the Traeger. I've always liked salmon, but now that I have made it on the Traeger, I crave it. The versatility of the Traeger allows you to make salmon that remains as moist as if you had baked it, yet full of that grill flavor. This is a must for anyone who enjoys salmon but has been fearful of putting it on the grill.

1 (3- to 4-lb [1.4- to 1.8-kg]) salmon fillet, with or without skin

Lemon-Garlic Butter Sauce

2 tbsp (28 g) unsalted butter

4 cloves garlic, minced

¼ cup (60 ml) lemon juice

3 tbsp (45 ml) honey

1 tsp reduced-sodium soy sauce

2 tsp (10 g) Dijon mustard

1 tbsp (4 g) chopped fresh parsley, plus more to serve

1 tsp salt

2 tsp onion powder

1 tsp paprika

½ tsp black pepper

Parmesan Topping

½ cup (35 g) Italian bread crumbs

3 tbsp (45 ml) melted butter

½ cup (40 g) grated Parmesan cheese

Preheat the Traeger to 275°F (135°C); see Note.

To make a pouch to cook the salmon in, roll out a piece of foil that extends inches past the length of your salmon (so you can fold up the sides). Lightly spray the foil with nonstick cooking spray. Place the salmon in the center of the foil (skin-side down if it has skin) and fold up all the sides of the foil snugly around the salmon.

To make the butter sauce, add the butter and the minced garlic to a medium bowl and microwave until the butter is melted. Whisk in the lemon juice, honey, soy sauce, mustard, parsley, salt, onion powder, paprika and pepper and pour evenly all over the salmon.

To make the Parmesan topping, whisk together the bread crumbs, butter and Parmesan until the butter is evenly absorbed. Pat the topping evenly over the salmon.

Place your salmon, in its pouch, on the grate of the Traeger for 60 minutes or until the internal temperature reaches 165°F (75°C).

Garnish with fresh parsley if desired and additional salt and pepper as needed. Serve immediately.

Note: When cooking seafood, we like to use fruitwood. Apple or cherry is preferred for this recipe.

HONEY-CHILI GRILLED SHRIMP

COOK TIME: 8 MINUTES · YIELD: 6–8 SERVINGS

Every time I grill shrimp I always wonder why I don't do it more often—it is so easy to make and there are so many different flavor profiles to try. This honey-chili shrimp is the perfect quick and easy recipe for those entertaining a house party or for those busy weeknights when you don't feel like spending a lot of time in the kitchen. The ease of setup and use of the Traeger makes this a super fun and quick meal.

Marinade

2 tbsp (17 g) minced garlic

1 tsp ground ginger

⅔ cup (160 ml) honey

3 tbsp (45 ml) fresh lemon juice

1 tbsp (15 ml) rice vinegar

1 tbsp (15 ml) low-sodium soy sauce

4 tsp (20 g) Asian chili paste

¼ cup (60 ml) olive oil

½ tsp salt

¼ tsp black pepper

1½ lb (680 g) 16/20–count shrimp, peeled and deveined

To make the marinade, in a medium bowl, whisk together the garlic, ginger, honey, lemon juice, rice vinegar, soy sauce and chili paste. Put a ½ cup (120 ml) of the mixture into a large freezer bag along with the olive oil, salt and pepper. Add the shrimp to the bag and massage to evenly coat. Place the bag in the refrigerator for 1 hour. Refrigerate the remaining marinade separately.

Set up your Traeger to run at 400°F (205°C). Drain the shrimp and discard the marinade. Thread the shrimp onto skewers.

Place the shrimp skewers directly on the grate of the grill and cook for 3 to 5 minutes on each side, or until shrimp has become pink and firm, being careful to not overcook.

Remove the shrimp from the grill and brush the shrimp with the reserved marinade. Serve any remaining marinade on the side as a dip.

MANGO CHIMICHURRI SKIRT STEAK

COOK TIME: 10 MINUTES · YIELD: 6–8 SERVINGS

Based on a dish you will find in many Brazilian steak houses, this recipe packs a lot of bold flavors. Rich and full of flavor on its own, a skirt steak cooks quickly, making it a perfect cut of beef for those who like good-quality meat but don't have an ample amount of time for cooking.

Marinade

½ cup (120 ml) olive oil

2 tbsp (30 ml) Worcestershire sauce

2 tbsp (30 ml) lime juice

2 tbsp (30 ml) lemon juice

6 cloves garlic, minced

1 tbsp (8 g) chili powder

1 tbsp (6 g) dried cumin

1- to 2-lb (454- to 908-g) skirt steak, trimmed

Mango Chimichurri

¼ cup (4 g) packed flat-leaf parsley

½ cup (8 g) packed cilantro

1 shallot, peeled

2 cloves garlic, peeled

2 mangos, peeled, pitted and finely chopped

½ cup (120 ml) olive oil

2 tbsp (30 ml) white vinegar

Salt and pepper to taste

To make the marinade, in a medium bowl, whisk together the olive oil, Worcestershire sauce, lime juice, lemon juice, garlic, chili powder and cumin and pour into a plastic freezer bag or shallow container. Add the skirt steak and marinate for at least 6 hours or preferably overnight in the refrigerator.

To make the chimichurri, finely chop the parsley, cilantro, shallot and garlic in a food processor. Scrape into a bowl and stir in the mangos, olive oil, vinegar, salt and pepper. Allow the mixture to sit, covered, for 2 to 4 hours before serving to allow flavors to meld. You can also make the chimichurri the day before; after marinating, chill in the refrigerator, then allow to return to room temperature before serving.

Set your Traeger to run at the highest setting. Let it run for 15 minutes to preheat properly. Remove the steak from the marinade and dry with a paper towel. Grill for 5 minutes per side or until an internal temperature of 140°F (60°C) is achieved.

Transfer the steak to a cutting board and loosely tent it with foil and let it rest for 5 to 10 minutes. Slice across the grain and top with the mango chimichurri.

BLACKENED FISH TACOS

COOK TIME: 8 MINUTES · YIELD: 4 SERVINGS

I happened to stop by the famed Duke's restaurant in Malibu, California, during one of their happy hours. On special were Bloody Marys and fish tacos. I have been ordering fish tacos at restaurants ever since and still have not found the magic that I tasted that day. So I worked on a recipe of my own to replicate the flavor I desired. Now you can have a taco just as tasty as the one I had there.

Marinade

3 tbsp (45 ml) olive oil

3 tbsp (45 ml) lime juice

1 tbsp (15 ml) reduced-sodium soy sauce

2 tbsp (18 g) Seafood Rub (page 141)

1½ lb (680 g) tilapia or 4 (5-oz [142-g]) filets

Avocado Cream

1 avocado, peeled and pitted

⅓ cup (80 g) sour cream

¼ cup (58 g) mayonnaise

1 tbsp (15 ml) lime juice

½ tsp salt

½ tsp ground cumin

Pineapple Cucumber Slaw

2 cups (330 g) chopped fresh pineapple

2 cups (140 g) thinly sliced red cabbage

1 medium cucumber, peeled and chopped

¼ cup (40 g) chopped red onion

½ cup (8 g) loosely packed cilantro, chopped

1 tbsp (15 ml) lime juice

Salt and pepper to taste

For Serving

2 tbsp (30 ml) olive oil

1 tbsp (14 g) butter

8 (6-inch [15-cm]) corn tortillas, warmed

½ cup (56 g) Mexican cheese blend

To make the marinade, combine the olive oil, lime juice, soy sauce and rub in a medium bowl. Add the marinade to a large freezer bag along with the fish. Marinate at room temperature for 30 minutes.

To make the avocado cream, add the avocado, sour cream, mayonnaise, lime juice, salt and cumin to a blender and blend until smooth, scraping down the sides as needed. Refrigerate in an airtight container until ready to serve.

To make the slaw, add the pineapple, cabbage, cucumber, onion, cilantro, lime juice, salt and pepper to a large bowl. Toss to combine. Refrigerate until ready to serve.

When ready to cook, start your Traeger and set the temperature to HIGH (450°F [230°C]), and preheat, lid closed, for 10 to 15 minutes. When the grill has come to temperature, place a cast-iron skillet on the grill, add the olive oil to the skillet, then close the lid of the grill and preheat it for 10 minutes. When the oil is very hot, add the butter. As soon as it melts, add the filets and cook for approximately 4 minutes per side, or until nicely blackened.

Remove the fish from the skillet and break into large pieces. Evenly divide the fish among the tortillas, then top with the cheese, slaw and avocado cream.

SPANISH GRILLED FISH
on Ciabatta

COOK TIME: 5 MINUTES · YIELD: 6 SERVINGS

This dish is . . . simply amazing. I was first introduced to this plate at a dear friend's house. She had friends visiting from the Galicia region of Spain who offered to cook a traditional Galician dinner for us. What I didn't know was that I was about to embark on one of the most flavorful home-cooked meals I've ever had. This recipe calls for sardines. No, not the ones in a can, but the larger (about 6 inches [15 cm] in length), fresh kind. They usually come cleaned and gutted, or you can ask the fish mongers to prep them for you. If you cannot find these at your local fish market, ask the fish monger to suggest a substitute.

4 cloves garlic, chopped

½ cup (120 ml) extra virgin olive oil, divided

Juice from 2 lemons (about ¼ cup [60 ml])

1 tsp smoked paprika

6 fresh whole sardines (about 1 lb [454 g]), scaled and gutted

1 large ciabatta bread

2 tbsp (1 g) chopped fresh parsley

Coarse sea salt and fresh black pepper to taste

Combine the garlic, ¼ cup (60 ml) of the olive oil, the lemon juice and paprika in a shallow baking dish. Add the sardines and flip to coat all sides with the marinade. Spoon some marinade into the cavity of the fish. Set the fish aside to marinate for 30 minutes.

Prepare your Traeger to run on HIGH.

Slice the ciabatta bread into 1-inch (3-cm) slices and grill until just crispy and grill marks appear.

Remove the fish from the marinade and grill the fish on the Traeger for 2 to 3 minutes per side, until charred.

Place each fish on a slice of the grilled bread. Drizzle generously with the remaining olive oil, sprinkle with the fresh parsley and season with salt and pepper to taste.

BURNT END AND BACON-WRAPPED POCKET BURGER

COOK TIME: 1½ HOURS · YIELD: 4 SERVINGS

Stuffed burgers are everywhere from mail order to your local grocery store. Save your money and wow your friends with a creative design of your own. We love this recipe—any time you can combine brisket, bacon and cheese with a burger you are going to be in nirvana.

2 lb (908 g) ground chuck (80/20 blend)

½ cup (72 g) your favorite BBQ rub, divided (see pages 133–141)

4 pieces thinly sliced raw bacon

8 oz (227 g) leftover brisket burnt ends or fatty brisket

8 oz (227 g) shredded sharp cheddar cheese

4 burger buns

In a medium bowl, add the ground chuck and ¼ cup (36 g) of the rub. Combine, but don't overwork the meat. Divide the meat into four equal-size balls. If you have one, use a scale to make sure the balls are even. Use your hands to round the meat into a ball using the bottom of a shot glass or your thumbs. Press the glass (or your thumb) into the center of the meat and use your hands to form the meat around the bottom of the glass, creating a well. It may break a little around the edges; gently fix any breaks with your hands.

Wrap a thin slice of bacon around the outside of the meat. Gently hold the meat with one hand to maintain its shape and remove the glass. Add a teaspoon of the remaining rub to the pocket in the beef. Repeat for the other three balls of meat.

Coarsely chop the burnt ends or fatty brisket and separate into four even piles. Stuff each pocket in the burger with the brisket and top each with 2 ounces (57 g) of cheese.

Meanwhile, prepare your Traeger to run at 225°F (110°C); see Note.

Place the burgers on the grate and allow them to cook for about 1½ hours or until the burgers reach an internal temperature of 160°F (70°C). Serve immediately on the buns.

Note: We prefer to use hickory pellets for our burgers. The deep smoky flavor seems to balance out the salty and savory flavors of the bacon and brisket.

HERB-RUBBED LAMB CHOPS

COOK TIME: 5 MINUTES • YIELD: 4 APPETIZER OR 2 DINNER SERVINGS

There's something so indulgent about a delicate, tender lamb chop. At home, I really enjoy eating them with my hands and cleaning the chop right down to the bone. The meat is so soft and each bite very flavorful. You can experiment with different types of herbs, but my favorite combination is simple yet powerful herbs you can easily find in your garden or local grocery store: parsley, oregano and thyme. If you're using dried herbs, cut the measurements down by a third (for example, 1 tablespoon of fresh oregano is equal to 1 teaspoon dried oregano).

3 cloves garlic

2 sprigs rosemary

2 tbsp (1 g) chopped fresh parsley

1 tbsp (1 g) chopped fresh oregano

1 tbsp (1 g) chopped fresh thyme

¼ cup (60 ml) olive oil

1 rack of lamb (about 8 chops)

Salt and pepper to taste

In a food processor or blender, combine the garlic, rosemary, parsley, oregano, thyme and olive oil until a smooth paste forms.

Slice the lamb into individual chops. Some people like to trim away all the fat from the long part of the bone, but I find that to be quite tasty so I leave it on. Sprinkle both sides of the lamb with salt and pepper. Rub the herb mixture onto the lamb chops and set aside to marinate for 1 hour.

Prepare your Traeger to run on HIGH.

Grill the chops on the Traeger with the lid open for 2 minutes, then flip and cook the chops another 3 minutes on the other side. Chops will be 145°F (62°C) for medium rare, or 160°F (70°C) for medium. Allow the chops to rest 5 minutes before serving.

DRUNKEN PINEAPPLE

COOK TIME: 4–8 MINUTES · YIELD: 6 SERVINGS

This dessert is great for when you want a little something sweet to end the meal, but aren't in the mood for anything heavy. Also, pineapple aids in digestion so if you've slightly overdone it at dinner, this might help you feel a little better about life. This recipe is almost effortless and you can even prepare it ahead of time by mixing the glaze in a sealed container.

½ cup (120 ml) spiced rum

2 tbsp (28 g) butter, melted

2 tsp (2 g) ground cinnamon

1 (20-oz [567-g]) can sliced pineapple, drained, or 1 fresh pineapple, cored and cut into ½-inch (13-mm) slices

1 pt (272 g) butter pecan or vanilla bean ice cream, optional

Prepare your Traeger to run on HIGH.

In a small bowl, combine the rum, melted butter and cinnamon and mix until well combined.

Dip each pineapple slice into the melted butter mixture and grill on your Traeger until slightly charred, 2 to 4 minutes per side.

If you want to dress it up, layer two slices of pineapple on a plate for each serving and top with a scoop of ice cream, if desired.

SMASHED BERRY GRILLED POUND CAKE

COOK TIME: 20 MINUTES · YIELD: 6 SERVINGS

Growing up in our household you could always find pound cake on the table after a meal. If you wanted dessert, it was pound cake and fruit with always fresh (never store bought) whipped cream. In my underdeveloped culinary mind, this was a boring dessert . . . the norm if you will. Nowadays fresh whipped cream is a treat and I serve my variation of this dessert quite often. There are never leftovers!

Bourbon Whipped Cream

1 cup (240 ml) heavy whipping cream

2 tbsp (16 g) powdered sugar

2 tbsp (30 ml) high-quality bourbon

Berry Topping

4 cups (1 kg) fresh or frozen berries of choice (I like strawberries, blueberries and raspberries), chopped

3 tbsp (38 g) granulated sugar

1 tbsp (15 ml) lemon juice

1 pound cake, cut into 6 slices

Prepare your Traeger to run on HIGH.

To make the whipped cream, pour the heavy whipping cream into a medium bowl and with a handheld mixer, whip until soft peaks form (or use an electric mixer). Gradually add in the powdered sugar, whipping until soft peaks form. Gently fold in the bourbon. Place the bowl in the refrigerator until ready to serve.

To make the berry topping, in a small saucepan, combine the berries, granulated sugar and lemon juice. Place the pan on the smoker grates and let the mixture come to a boil. When the mixture is boiling, cook, stirring often and mashing with a wooden spoon to break down the berries, for about 10 minutes, until it has a syrup-like consistency. Remove the pot from the smoker.

Place the slices of pound cake onto the smoker grates and grill for about 2 minutes per side until grill marks are visible. Carefully flip the cake and grill the other side. Remove the cake from the smoker and place on a plate. Layer with a few spoonfuls of the berry topping, followed by a generous dollop of whipped cream. Serve immediately.

Note: If you have little ones, omit the bourbon in the whipped cream.

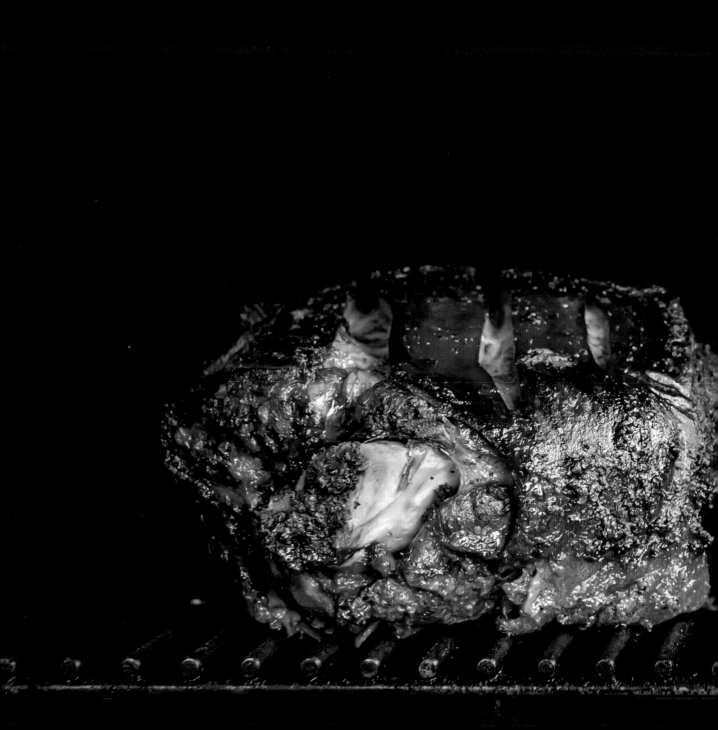

FROM *the* OVEN

BARBECUE ENTHUSIASM SEEMS TO BE GROWING EVERY YEAR.

Many homeowners, no longer content with burgers and hot dogs, are venturing into barbecue. I've long been an advocate for pellet smokers, and the equipment available for the homeowner is finally available. The Traeger offers a versatility that very few barbecue appliances can. We have become accustomed to our equipment being able to smoke and grill. However, the Traeger's ability to be used as an oven is what really sets it apart, in my opinion. This versatility allows you to be creative in ways you haven't thought of before when using your grill.

BALSAMIC-GLAZED ROASTED BRUSSELS SPROUTS

with Bacon

COOK TIME: 1½ HOURS · YIELD: 6 SERVINGS

Here's a chance to make something healthy with your bacon! This recipe produces tasty sweet and salty Brussels sprouts that will run alongside any protein that's next to it. This bold-tasting sprout pairs well with pork chops and steaks and won't just be a veggie that gets lost on your plate. I find that I can never quite make enough of these, as everyone goes back for seconds and thirds.

1 lb (454 g) Brussels sprouts

4 slices bacon

3 cloves garlic, minced

1½ tbsp (13 g) dry rub (see pages 133–141)

1 cup (240 ml) balsamic vinegar

½ cup (100) granulated sugar

Prepare your Traeger to run at the highest temperature.

Trim the stem ends off the Brussels sprouts and cut them in half lengthwise. Place a cast-iron pan directly on the smoker grates and cook the bacon until crisp. Remove the bacon and place it on a paper towel, leaving the bacon grease in the pan. Reduce the smoker to 250°F (120°C).

Add the garlic and Brussels sprouts to the cast-iron pan and sprinkle with the rub. Toss to coat and close the lid of the smoker. Smoke for 1 hour, or until the Brussels sprouts are fork tender.

Chop the bacon and set aside.

To make the balsamic glaze, combine the balsamic vinegar and sugar in a small saucepan over high heat. When the mixture is gently boiling, reduce the heat to medium-low and let simmer, stirring occasionally, for 10 minutes. The balsamic glaze is finished when it coats the back of a spoon.

Add the glaze mixture to the Brussels sprouts and toss to coat them, then smoke another 10 minutes. Add the chopped bacon to the pan and toss.

CANDIED MAPLE BACON

COOK TIME: 40–60 MINUTES • YIELD: 15–20 SERVINGS

During the holidays, I like to have this Candied Maple Bacon in a Mason jar on our bar alongside our Sweet n' Spicy Smoked Pecans (page 125). This treat is not only delicious but it looks great and is incredibly easy to make, with only three ingredients. It can be eaten as is or chopped up and used as a topping for ice cream, sweet potato casserole, salad or pie. The maple syrup and brown sugar baste the bacon as it smokes, creating a beautifully caramelized, sweet, crunchy coating. The candied bacon can be stored in an airtight container on the counter for up to a week, but I doubt it'll make it that long without being devoured!

½ cup (110 g) dark brown sugar

½ cup (120 ml) Grade A maple syrup

1 lb (454 g) bacon

Prepare your Traeger to run at 300°F (150°C). Line a baking sheet with parchment paper.

In a bowl, mix the brown sugar and syrup until combined. Lay the bacon in a single layer on the prepared baking sheet and brush generously with the sugar mixture. Flip the bacon and repeat on the other side.

Place the baking sheet with the bacon in the smoker and close the lid. After 20 minutes, flip the bacon and let it cook another 15 to 20 minutes until the sugar is melted and the bacon is cooked (note that the bacon will not be crispy when you remove it from the smoker).

Remove the pan from the smoker and let the bacon sit in the pan another 10 to 15 minutes to harden and finish the candying process. Remove the bacon from the pan and place in Mason jars or on a plate to serve.

CHICKEN SKIN CRACKLINGS

COOK TIME: 30–45 MINUTES · YIELD: 6 SERVINGS

These snacks take the tastiest part of the chicken to an entirely other level. In my house, the crispy skin of the chicken is the overall favorite and is often gone before the chicken hits the dinner table. Made correctly, these skins have the consistency of a potato chip and the savory flavor of well-seasoned chicken. This recipe is incredibly easy, with just two ingredients.

2 whole chickens, 3 to 4 lb (1.4 to 1.8 g) each, skin on, or 8 lb (3.6 kg) chicken thighs, skin on

1 tbsp (9 g) poultry rub

Prepare your Traeger to run at 350°F (175°C).

To remove the skin from the chicken, place the chicken on a cutting board. Gently lift up one end of the skin and peel it back, separating the thin layer of fat between the chicken meat and the skin as you pull. Save the chicken meat for use in another recipe.

Slice your skins into 1-inch (3-cm)-long by ½-inch (13-mm)-wide strips. Pat the chicken skin dry with a paper towel.

Line a baking sheet with parchment paper and place the chicken skins on the baking sheet. Stretch the chicken skins so they lay flat. Sprinkle lightly with the poultry rub.

Place the baking sheet in the smoker and close the lid. Let the skins bake for 30 to 45 minutes, until brown and crisp. Let cool and enjoy right away, or store in an airtight container on the counter for up to 3 days.

CUBAN-STYLE PORK SHOULDER

COOK TIME: 6–7 HOURS · YIELD: 8 SERVINGS

Whether you call it pork butt, pork shoulder or Boston butt, it's all the same. It's one of the first things new pitmasters try their hand at making, probably due to the fact that it's one of the easiest and cheapest meats to smoke. You can cook it for what seems like days and it won't dry out due to its high fat content. It can also take on a variety of flavors depending on what you rub it with and which sauce you use. So instead of sharing a traditional pork butt recipe, I'd like to give you a Cuban-style shredded pork. Most commonly used in a Cuban sandwich or served alongside yellow rice and pigeon beans, "pernil," as it's called, is traditionally a slow-roasted, marinated pork shoulder. Plan accordingly, as this recipe calls for the pork to marinate overnight.

15 cloves garlic, peeled

2 tbsp (30 ml) olive oil, plus more if needed

2 tsp (12 ml) white vinegar

2 tbsp (30 ml) adobo

1 tbsp (3 g) dried oregano

1 large orange, peeled

1 medium onion (white, yellow, Spanish or sweet), peeled

2 packets Goya Sazón con Culantro y Achiote

8 to 10 lb (3.6 to 4.5 kg) pork shoulder, bone in, skin on

2 tbsp (36 g) salt

2 tbsp (14 g) black pepper

Place the garlic, olive oil, vinegar, adobo, dried oregano, orange, onion and Sazón in a blender. Pulse until the mixture is well blended, stopping every few seconds to scrape down the sides. Add more olive oil as needed to obtain a paste-like consistency. Remove the pork from its packaging, rinse and pat dry. Rub with the salt and pepper to lightly coat.

Using the tip of a chef's knife, stab 15 to 20 slices, about 1 inch (3 cm) deep and 1 inch (3 cm) wide, through the skin and into the meat of the pork shoulder. Place the pork, skin-side up, in a disposable aluminum half-size tray. Using your hands, rub the marinade mixture all over the pork and into the slices. Cover and refrigerate the pork shoulder 24 to 48 hours.

When it's ready to cook, remove the pork shoulder from the refrigerator and let it rest 30 minutes on the counter. Meanwhile, preheat your Traeger to 325°F (165°C).

Using a spoon, scrape off any seasonings on the skin of the pork shoulder and put the scrapings in the bottom of the roasting pan. Cover the pork loosely with aluminum foil and cook in your Traeger for 5 to 6 hours, or until the internal temperature reaches 180°F (82°C). The pork should be fork tender at this point. Increase the temperature on your Traeger to HIGH and roast 20 to 30 minutes longer, checking every 10 minutes until the skin is crispy.

Let the pork rest for 20 minutes. Remove the skin and slice it up for cracklings. Shred the pork meat and serve with the cracklings alongside rice and beans, or as a Cuban sandwich, or by itself!

PIZZA FATTY

COOK TIME: 1 HOUR · YIELD: 6 SERVINGS

This sausage fatty is often requested for weeknight dinners from my kids because it's a play on two very familiar flavors: pizza and meatloaf. The use of the mozzarella and marinara give it a flavor that reminds us of pizza, and the ground sausage gives it the texture of a traditional meatloaf. I like to make this ahead and have it ready in the fridge or freezer for nights I want a smoked dinner but don't have the extra time to prep something. The recipe for this sausage fatty does not call for the bacon weave, but feel free to add it if you'd like!

2 lb (908 g) ground Italian sausage sweet or hot, your choice (without casing)

2 tsp (2 g) Italian seasoning

½ tsp salt

½ tsp black pepper

1 cup (240 ml) marinara sauce, divided

1 cup (115 g) shredded mozzarella cheese

Prepare your Traeger to run at 350°F (175°C).

On a long piece of plastic wrap, spread out the sausage into an 8 x 8–inch (20 x 20–cm) square, patting down gently and keeping the same thickness throughout the layer (so it will cook evenly). Sprinkle the Italian seasoning, salt and pepper evenly over the sausage. Cover the sausage with a ½ cup (120 ml) of the marinara sauce, then the mozzarella cheese.

Carefully begin rolling the sausage into a log, using the plastic wrap to lift and guide the sausage if necessary. Make sure the mozzarella and sauce filling stay inside the sausage. Try to seal any holes and pinch off the ends. The sausage should now be in the shape of a log. At this point, if you are saving this fatty for another day, wrap it tightly in plastic wrap and put it in the refrigerator or freezer. If you are cooking your pizza fatty immediately, place it in a disposable aluminum tray.

Place the tray directly on the smoker grates and close the lid. After 45 minutes, open the smoker door and spoon the rest of the marinara sauce over your sausage, and cover with aluminum foil. Allow the sausage to cook another 10 to 15 minutes, or until an instant-read thermometer inserted into the center of the roll reads 165°F (75°C).

Remove the pan from the smoker and allow the sausage to cool for 5 minutes. Using a sharp knife, slice the roll into ½-inch (13-mm)-thick pieces.

APPLE-GLAZED PORK LOIN

COOK TIME: 45–60 MINUTES · YIELD: 6 SERVINGS

Pork loin is an extremely versatile piece of meat that will take on whatever flavor you throw at it. Brining it gives this large piece of meat a tender bite and depth of flavor you just can't get by seasoning alone. Growing up, pork chops and applesauce were a weeknight dinner staple, so I tried to create something similar but much more flavorful in this recipe.

3½ cups (840 ml) apple juice or apple cider, divided

2 tbsp (28 g) brown sugar

1 cup (240 ml) water

2 tbsp (36 g) salt

1 tbsp (7 g) ground black pepper

2½ to 3 lb (1.1 to 1.4 kg) pork loin, boneless

½ cup (120 ml) honey

2 tbsp (30 g) Dijon mustard

1 sweet apple

¼ cup (36 g) BBQ rub (see pages 133–141)

In a saucepan, combine 2 cups (480 ml) of the apple juice, the brown sugar, water, salt and pepper. Warm the mixture on the stove over medium heat just until the sugar and salt are dissolved. Cool the brine to room temperature and put it in a resealable plastic bag. Add the pork loin to the bag and put it in the refrigerator. Allow the loin to sit in the mixture for 1 to 2 hours.

While the pork is brining, prepare the glaze. In a medium saucepan, combine the remaining 1½ cups (360 ml) of apple juice, honey and mustard and heat over medium heat about 5 minutes, until slightly thickened.

Core the apple, then slice into ¼-inch (6-mm) rings.

Remove the loin from the bag and discard the brine. Place the loin in a disposable aluminum tray and cover it on all sides with the rub, then the glaze mixture. Lay the sliced apples over the top of the loin.

Meanwhile, prepare your Traeger to run at 275°F (135°C).

Place the tray in your preheated Traeger and smoke for 45 minutes to 1 hour, or until the internal temperature reads 145°F (62°C). Allow the loin to rest for 5 minutes before slicing.

SAUSAGE-STUFFED PORTOBELLO MUSHROOMS

COOK TIME: 10–15 MINUTES · YIELD: 6 SERVINGS

These sausage-stuffed portobello mushrooms are great for an appetizer or lunch. Portobello mushrooms are naturally hearty and with the addition of sausage and cheese, you have yourself a meal. Pretty much any shredded cheese will work for this recipe; I typically use whatever is in the fridge, which usually happens to be cheddar or mozzarella.

6 portobello mushroom caps

Olive oil, for brushing

Salt and pepper to taste

1½ lb (680 g) sweet or hot Italian ground sausage, without casing

1 tsp garlic powder

1 tsp oregano

1 medium yellow onion, finely chopped

1 cup (115 g) shredded cheese

Preheat your Traeger to 350°F (175°C).

Clean the mushroom caps by removing the stems and scraping out the gills. Wipe the caps with a damp paper towel. Place the mushroom caps on a baking sheet, brush with olive oil and season both sides with salt and pepper.

In a medium skillet over medium heat, add the sausage, garlic powder and oregano and cook about 5 minutes, until browned. Add the chopped onion and cook 3 minutes more, until the onion is softened. Remove the sausage mixture from the heat and spoon evenly into each of the portobello mushrooms, then top each one with equal amounts of the shredded cheese.

Place the mushrooms carefully on the smoker grates and cook 10 to 15 minutes, until the mushrooms are tender.

THE DEVIL'S BLT
(Bacon, Lobster, Tomato) Sliders

COOK TIME: 15–17 MINUTES • YIELD: 8 SLIDERS

I've always loved lobster meat but dislike all the work to get it out of the shell while trying to eat. So, I came up with my own take on a lobster roll. I've made these sliders dozens of times and have yet to have anyone say they are *no bueno*; even my non–crustacean–loving friends enjoy them. I've also served the bacon to be added as a condiment when feeding my pescatarian friends.

5 (5- to 6-oz [142- to 170-g]) lobster tails

2 tbsp (30 ml) olive oil

½ cup (72 g) Seafood Rub (page 141), divided

8 oz (227 g) salted butter

1 lb (454 g) cooked and crumbled bacon

Light mayo, to taste

8 potato roll sliders

1 cup (150 g) cherry tomatoes, chopped

Prepare your Traeger to run at 350°F (175°C).

Using kitchen shears, cut down the middle of the back of the lobster tail. Using your finger, loosen the meat inside the shell and pull it up through the cut opening but don't pull the meat all the way off the shell. The lobster meat will rest on top of its shell and act as its own roasting pan. Place the tails on a rack set in a sheet pan, lightly coat the meat with olive oil and sprinkle with Seafood Rub.

Cook the tails about 2 minutes per ounce, 10 to 12 minutes. Remove the tails from the Traeger and set the smoker to HIGH. Preheat for 5 minutes.

Place a pat of butter on each tail and place the tails back in the Traeger for 5 minutes. Remove, let cool, remove the meat from the shell and chop.

To construct the sliders, in a bowl, mix the chopped lobster meat, bacon and mayo (use an amount to your liking—some people like wet lobster rolls and others dry; I personally think less is best). Put a scoop of the lobster mixture on a slider bun, lightly sprinkle it with some of the Seafood Rub and top with a few tomato pieces.

PROTEIN POWER QUICHE
with Chicken and Spinach

COOK TIME: 45 MINUTES • YIELD: 6 SLICES

This is a great go-to breakfast, especially the morning after a good cookout when your houseguests decided to stay over and you all need a little something extra to get you going for the day. This quiche is simple, quick and packed with nutrients. It pairs extremely well with the Blueberry Sausage Fatty (page 29). I'm a big fan of nutmeg and in this recipe I think it adds a nice balance and taste, eliminating the need for salt and pepper.

1¼ cups (175 g) cooked chicken, chopped (leftovers recommended)

1 cup (30 g) chopped baby spinach

¾ cup (85 g) shredded cheddar cheese

1 store-bought frozen piecrust

4 egg whites or Egg Beaters (equivalent to 4 eggs)

¾ cup (180 ml) skim milk

½ cup (96 g) light sour cream or yogurt

½ tsp nutmeg

Prepare your Traeger to run at 350°F (175°C).

In a large bowl, combine the chicken, spinach and cheddar cheese and transfer to the piecrust.

Whisk the egg whites, milk, sour cream and nutmeg together until combined and pour into the piecrust.

Place the quiche in the smoker for about 45 minutes or until a knife comes out clean. Slice into 6 pieces and serve.

COCONUT-CARAMEL SWEET POTATOES

COOK TIME: 1 HOUR • YIELD: 4 SERVINGS

These sweet potatoes go great with chicken or fish, and the coconut-caramel sauce is the perfect balance of sweet and salty. This dish is indigenous to Hawaii and is a delicious twist on a classic favorite without feeling too unfamiliar. The taste will remind you of a sweet potato casserole but with a more savory, rich flavor profile.

4 medium sweet potatoes

1 (13.5-oz [383-g]) can full-fat coconut milk

⅓ cup (80 ml) maple syrup

¼ cup (55 g) brown sugar

½ tsp salt

1 tsp vanilla extract

1 tsp coconut oil

8 tbsp (112 g) salted butter, softened

Prepare your Traeger to run at 375°F (190°C).

Rinse the sweet potatoes well, removing any dirt, and pat dry. Pierce the potatoes with a fork in several places so they will vent while cooking. Place the sweet potatoes directly on the smoker grate and close the lid for 1 hour.

While the potatoes are cooking, in a medium saucepan, combine the coconut milk, syrup, brown sugar and salt over medium-high heat until just boiling. Reduce the heat and simmer for 25 minutes, stirring occasionally. Increase the heat slightly and stir often, making sure to scrape the bottom and sides of the saucepan to remove the browned bits. Continue this process for 5 to 10 minutes until the sauce is a caramel color and thickened enough that it will coat the back of a spoon. Remove the sauce from the stove and stir in the vanilla extract and coconut oil.

Check the sweet potatoes after 1 hour; they should be soft when done. If not done, check every 5 minutes.

Remove the sweet potatoes from the smoker and slice each top lengthwise and squeeze to open. Top each sweet potato with 2 tablespoons (28 g) of the softened butter and spoon the coconut-caramel mixture over the top of each potato. Serve warm.

CHIPOTLE CORN WHIPS

COOK TIME: 20–30 MINUTES · YIELD: 6 SERVINGS

This recipe produces a creamy, savory and smoky flavor due to the chipotle peppers, and it can be made on the stove or in the Traeger set to HIGH. The peppers can be found in a can in your local grocery's Spanish aisle.

3 lb (1.4 kg) russet potatoes

¾ cup (180 ml) heavy cream

5 tbsp (70 g) salted butter, divided

1 tsp kosher salt, plus more as needed

2 cups (300 g) kernels sweet corn

2 tbsp (34 g) chipotle peppers in adobo sauce, minced (from approximately 2 peppers); see Note

⅓ cup (80 g) sour cream

Prepare your Traeger to run on HIGH.

Cut the potatoes, unpeeled, evenly into approximately 1-inch (3-cm) cubes. Place the potatoes in a medium saucepan and cover with about 2 inches (5 cm) of cold, salted water. Place the pot on the smoker grates, close the lid and bring to a boil. Once the water is boiling, cook for 15 minutes.

While the potatoes are boiling, warm the cream and 4 tablespoons (56 g) of the butter until the butter is melted. Set the mixture aside.

In a separate pan over medium heat, warm the remaining 1 tablespoon (14 g) of butter and add a pinch of salt. When the butter is melted, sauté the corn for 5 minutes, until warmed and slightly browned. Set the corn aside.

Once the potatoes have cooked for 15 minutes, remove from the heat, drain well, then return the potatoes to the pan. Slowly add the cream mixture to the potatoes while mixing with a hand mixer on the lowest setting. When the butter and cream begin to incorporate into the potatoes, add the teaspoon of salt, chipotle peppers and sour cream. Stop mixing as soon as all the ingredients come together and then fold in the sautéed corn by hand. Cover and let the mixture rest for 10 minutes before serving.

Note: For an added kick, drizzle some adobo sauce from the can of peppers on top before serving.

CHEDDAR CORNBREAD MADELEINE BITES

COOK TIME: 10 MINUTES • YIELD: 36 MADELEINES

This madeleine cornbread is an elegant take on the conventional cornbread. The use of corn flour in this recipe lends a softer, more delicate cake-like texture. Each madeleine is a luscious bite of sweet and savory goodness and they are addictingly delicious. I made these one afternoon hoping to have some for breakfast the next day . . . they never made it to morning. If you can't find metal madeleine pans, you can use a mini muffin pan. Plan accordingly, as this recipe needs to chill for 3 hours.

1 cup (226 g) unsalted butter, melted

2 tbsp (28 g) brown sugar

2 tbsp (30 ml) agave syrup

1¾ cups (200 g) corn flour (I like Bob's Red Mill)

1 cup (115 g) finely shredded cheddar cheese

1½ tsp (7 g) baking powder

½ tsp kosher salt

5 large eggs

½ cup (100 g) granulated sugar

1½ tsp (7 ml) vanilla extract

Cooking spray or oil

In a small bowl, mix the melted butter, brown sugar and agave with a spoon until combined.

In a separate medium bowl, mix the corn flour, cheese, baking powder and salt until combined.

Add the eggs, granulated sugar and vanilla extract to the melted butter mixture and beat on high speed for about 2 minutes, until fluffy. Stir in the corn flour mixture just until combined. Spoon the mixture into a gallon-size (3.8-L) freezer bag (to make it easier to pipe into pans later) and place the bag in the refrigerator to cool for 3 hours.

When ready to cook, prepare your Traeger to run at 350°F (175°C).

Lightly grease your madeleine or mini muffin pan with cooking spray or oil. Remove the dough from the fridge and cut a small corner off the bag. Pipe the batter into the pans through the corner of the bag. Fill the pans almost all the way to the top, place the pan on the smoker and close the lid. Cook for 5 to 10 minutes, until golden brown around the edges and the center of a madeleine springs back when touched.

Let the madeleines cool slightly and remove from the pan to start the next batch. Serve warm, cold, broken—they're delicious in any form!

ROASTED POTATOES
with Garlic Aioli

COOK TIME: 45 MINUTES · YIELD: 4 SERVINGS

Is there a side dish that better complements the main entrée than a potato? A potato is so versatile—from mashed to baked to fried, we all have our favorites. We have found that roasted fingerling potatoes are easy to make and will satisfy the heartiest of steak and potato eaters.

3 lb (1.4 kg) fingerling potatoes

1 cup (230 g) mayonnaise

½ cup (120 g) sour cream

⅓ cup (80 ml) lemon juice

½ tbsp (8 g) Dijon mustard

¼ cup (35 g) chopped garlic (about 5 cloves)

1 tbsp (2 g) chopped fresh tarragon

¾ tsp ground black pepper

Pinch of cayenne pepper

¼ tsp smoked paprika

Prepare your Traeger to run at 375°F (190°C).

Rinse and dry the potatoes and place them on a baking sheet in a single layer. Place the baking sheet in the smoker and close the lid. Cook for about 30 minutes (or until fork tender), turning the potatoes over halfway through the cooking process.

While the potatoes are cooking, prepare the aioli. Place the mayonnaise, sour cream, lemon juice, mustard, garlic, tarragon, black pepper and cayenne pepper in a blender. Blend on high until smooth.

Remove the potatoes from the smoker and allow them to cool slightly. Drizzle with the aioli mixture and sprinkle the smoked paprika on top.

ROASTED PRIME RIB
with Horseradish Crust

COOK TIME: 2 HOURS · YIELD: 8–10 SERVINGS

There is nothing more impressive to guests than taking a large prime rib roast off the grill.
This is a great dish for the holidays or any large family gathering.

1 (8-lb [3.6-kg]) bone-in prime rib beef roast, 4 ribs

6 cloves garlic

⅓ cup (80 g) grated horseradish

Leaves from 6 rosemary sprigs

Leaves from 6 thyme sprigs

½ cup (125 g) kosher salt

¼ cup (28 g) black pepper

½ cup (120 ml) olive oil

Preheat the Traeger to 350°F (175°C); see Note.

Lay the beef in a roasting pan, bone-side down.

In a food processor, blend together the garlic, horseradish, rosemary, thyme, salt, pepper and olive oil to make a paste. Generously apply the paste over the entire roast.

Put the pan on the Traeger and roast the beef until the internal temperature registers 125°F (52°C), approximately 2 hours. Remove the roast and let it rest for 20 minutes before carving.

Note: Beef loves smoke and can take a lot of it. For this recipe we like using hickory to provide a well-balanced smoky flavor.

PROVOLONE AND HERB-STUFFED CHICKEN ROLLUPS

COOK TIME: 30–45 MINUTES · YIELD: 4 SERVINGS

This is a simple weeknight dinner recipe that can be easily adjusted to accommodate a larger family, or smaller one. I like to double the recipe to have leftovers for lunch or dinner the next day. You can pair this with almost any side; some of my favorites are pasta and Roasted Parmesan Broccoli (page 122).

2 large chicken breasts

Garlic powder

Salt and pepper

½ cup (8 g) chopped fresh parsley

½ cup (21 g) chopped fresh basil

6 slices provolone cheese

6 slices bacon

Preheat your Traeger to run at 375°F (190°C).

Butterfly the chicken by slicing each breast horizontally, but not completely in half (like a book). Line a cutting board with plastic wrap and place one piece of chicken on it. Cover the chicken with one piece of plastic wrap and evenly pound the meat out to about ¼ inch (6 mm) thick. Repeat with the other breast. Remove the top plastic wrap and sprinkle both sides of the flattened breast with garlic powder, salt and pepper. Top each flattened breast with half of the chopped parsley, half of the chopped basil and three slices of provolone. Tightly roll the chicken using the bottom plastic wrap as a guide. Wrap each piece in three slices of bacon and secure by tying twine around the outside of the rolled breast.

Place the chicken in a disposable aluminum pan and in the preheated Traeger. Close the lid and check the chicken's internal temperature after 30 minutes. Remove when the internal temperature is 160°F (70°C) and let the meat rest for 10 minutes to finish cooking while retaining the juices.

Slice each breast into ½-inch (13-mm)-thick slices and drizzle with the pan drippings.

ROASTED PARMESAN BROCCOLI

COOK TIME: 20 MINUTES · YIELD: 4 SERVINGS

I love the flavor I can infuse into broccoli simply by slathering it in olive oil and spices. I like to modify this recipe depending on the protein I'm serving. For red meats I like to kick it up and add smoked paprika and chili powder to the olive oil bath, and for more delicate proteins such as fish and chicken I like to keep it simple with garlic powder, salt and pepper. You can also substitute the broccoli with cauliflower or roast them both together. This recipe goes to show you how versatile the Traeger can be—from roasting broccoli to baking up some brownies, this smoker really does it all.

½ cup (120 ml) olive oil

½ cup (40 g) grated Parmesan cheese

1 tbsp (10 g) garlic powder

1 tsp smoked paprika (optional)

1 tsp chili powder (optional)

Salt and pepper to taste

1 large head broccoli (about 2 lb [908 g]), stems removed, chopped into florets

Set your Traeger to run on HIGH.

In a large bowl, combine the olive oil, Parmesan cheese, garlic powder, paprika (if using), chili powder (if using), salt and pepper. Place the broccoli florets in the bowl and toss until evenly coated. Spread the broccoli on a sheet pan in a single layer, place in the smoker and close the lid.

After 10 minutes, flip the broccoli to crisp the other side. Close the lid and let the broccoli roast another 10 minutes or until both sides are slightly browned and crispy.

Serve warm.

SWEET N' SPICY SMOKED PECANS

COOK TIME: 1 HOUR · YIELD: 8 SERVINGS

In my household, we smoke food year-round. Living in the Northeast, that means in the frigid winters when 30°F (−1°C) temperatures are considered "warm." Oftentimes we kick up the heat in our food because it warms you from the inside out. This recipe was created as something for guests to snack on during the holidays, but truthfully we enjoy having these any time of the year.

We toast our pecans in the first step. Don't skip this step. This helps to bring forth a richer, nuttier flavor (think the difference between raw sugar versus caramelized sugar, or microwaved butter versus browned butter) and also ensures they stay crisp throughout the smoking process.

Stored in an airtight container, these will last for weeks (although I doubt they'll last that long without being eaten).

4 cups (440 g) pecans, shelled and halved

½ cup (120 ml) pure maple syrup

1 tbsp (15 ml) bourbon (or 1½ tsp [7 ml] vanilla extract)

2 tbsp (28 g) unsalted butter

1 tsp salt

½ tsp cayenne pepper

¼ tsp ground black pepper

1 large egg, at room temperature

Prepare your Traeger by turning it to the SMOKE setting, wait about 5 minutes for it to produce smoke, then set the Traeger to run at 350°F (175°C).

Spread the pecans in a full-size (20 x 12 inches [51 x 30 cm]) disposable aluminum tray and place in the smoker on the grates once it reaches the correct temperature. Toast the pecans for 10 minutes, mixing after 5 minutes to evenly toast.

Let the pecans cool and lower your Traeger to 250°F (120°C).

Meanwhile, place the syrup, bourbon, butter, salt, cayenne pepper and black pepper in a large bowl. Mix until well combined. In a different bowl, separate the egg, discard the yolk (or save for a later use) and whisk the white until light and frothy. Place the pecans in the large bowl with all ingredients except the egg white and mix until well coated. Add the egg white in last and gently mix. Spread the pecans back in the tray. Place the tray in the smoker and cook about 40 minutes.

Immediately loosen the pecans from the tray and allow them to cool for 10 minutes or until crisp. Enjoy!

SKILLET BOURBON BROWNIES

COOK TIME: 45 MINUTES · YIELD: 4–6 SERVINGS

These brownies are the perfect ending to a good cookout. Pellets make it so easy to get a fire going on your Traeger after you've done your cooking and shut off your smoker. You can throw these on the Traeger when everyone's almost done eating to have right after the meal, or wait a bit and have them at the end of the night with some good bourbon or a cup of coffee. You'll need a 10-inch (25-cm) cast-iron pan or four mini 3½-inch (9-cm) pans.

½ cup (63 g) all-purpose flour

¼ tsp baking soda

½ tsp salt

8 oz (227 g) dark chocolate, chopped

½ cup (114 g) unsalted butter, plus more for the pan

2 tbsp (30 ml) oil

3 large eggs

1 cup (220 g) packed brown sugar

¾ cup (150 g) granulated sugar

2 tsp (10 ml) vanilla extract or bourbon

1 recipe Bourbon Whipped Cream (page 88) or vanilla ice cream, for serving

Prepare your Traeger to run at 325°F (165°C) and preheat for 10 minutes while you prepare your batter.

In a medium bowl, combine the flour, baking soda and salt.

Place the chocolate, butter and oil in a microwave-safe bowl and microwave for 30 seconds, stir, then microwave in 15-second intervals until melted. Let the mixture cool slightly (about 5 minutes). Add the eggs, brown sugar, granulated sugar and vanilla and stir until combined. Add the flour mixture and stir just until the ingredients are combined.

Grease a cast-iron pan (or pans) with butter and pour in the batter. Place the pan(s) on the grates and close the lid for 40 minutes. After 40 minutes, insert a toothpick into the middle of the brownie. The toothpick should not be wet but will have some brownie bits. Remove the pan(s) from the smoker and allow to cool for about 10 minutes.

Slice the brownie into six wedges and top with the whipped cream or ice cream.

SMOKED APPLE PIE

COOK TIME: 75–80 MINUTES · YIELD: 6 SERVINGS

There's something so comforting and familiar about apple pie. It's always there for major holidays, whether it's in the summer for Independence Day, fall for Thanksgiving, or even during one of our winter holidays. It's a staple on the dessert table and generally enjoyed by all. However, in my household there is a divide over which apples produce the best pie: tart or sweet. So this combination of Granny Smith and Gala apples results in the perfect balance between sweet and tart. Feel free to use any apple combination you like; this specific combo is merely a suggestion.

2 (9-inch [23-cm]) piecrusts (homemade or store bought, no judgment here), defrosted if frozen

3 tart apples, such as Granny Smith, peeled, cored and cut into ¼-inch (6-mm) slices

3 sweet apples, such as Gala, peeled, cored and cut into ¼-inch (6-mm) slices

1 tbsp (15 ml) lemon juice

½ cup (110 g) brown sugar

¼ cup (31 g) all-purpose flour

1 tsp ground cinnamon

½ tsp ground nutmeg

1 egg

1 tsp water or milk

Prepare your Traeger to run on HIGH.

Line a 9-inch (23-cm) pie pan with one of the crusts. Place the pan on the Traeger grate, close the lid and cook for 15 to 20 minutes, until golden brown. Be sure to check after 15 minutes to be sure it does not burn.

Meanwhile, place the sliced apples in a large bowl and drizzle them with the lemon juice. Mix in the brown sugar, flour, cinnamon and nutmeg until well combined.

Remove the piecrust from the smoker (if you haven't already), then set your Traeger to run at 375°F (190°C).

Pour the apple mixture into the baked piecrust and top with the uncooked crust, crimping the sides. Cut a few slits in the top of the piecrust to vent the pie as it cooks.

In a small bowl, combine the egg and water and mix well. Brush the top of the pie evenly with the egg wash and place the pie in the smoker. Cook for 30 minutes, then check the pie for browning. If it's a nice golden brown, tent a piece of foil on top to prevent the top from burning and cook for another 30 minutes. If you have not tented the pie, check the pie every 10 minutes to be sure the crust does not burn.

Remove the pie from the smoker and allow to rest before slicing.

RUBS & SAUCES

THERE ARE LITERALLY HUNDREDS IF NOT THOUSANDS OF SPICES, rubs and sauces available for purchase at grocery stores, specialty shops and over the Internet. Some are good and some . . . well, not so good.

After a few successful cooks on your Traeger, you might want to try to develop your own flavor profile and make your own signature rub or seasoning. I'll try to give you a basic lesson in BBQ rubs and you can take it from there—the sky is the limit.

Historically, the cut of meat, cooking method and type of sauce would tell you which region of the USA your BBQ was from. From the Carolinas to Texas, the flavor of your sauce would define where your BBQ was created. However, while that might have worked for our forefathers, BBQ has seen a global explosion during the last decade. With so many flavors at our disposal, no longer does a flavor profile have to define a region; instead, a flavor profile can be used to define your personal style for your dish.

A quick note on salt and sugars: Kosher salt is preferred by most BBQ chefs because of its grain size and because it imparts less of a salty and iron flavor than regular table salt. Sugars most often used are brown sugar and in-the-raw turbinado sugar. The turbinado sugar has a high burn point, which is a reason it's a sugar of choice.

ALL-AROUND BBQ RUB

YIELD: ½ CUP (90 G)

A great all-around BBQ rub, this mix is good on just about anything from meat to vegetables.

2 tbsp (14 g) paprika

2 tbsp (20 g) granulated garlic

1 tbsp (18 g) kosher salt

1 tbsp (5 g) cayenne pepper

1 tbsp (7 g) black pepper

1 tbsp (14 g) turbinado sugar

1 tbsp (7 g) onion powder

1 tbsp (3 g) dried oregano

½ tbsp (1 g) dried thyme

Add the paprika, garlic, salt, cayenne and black pepper, sugar, onion powder, oregano and thyme to a small bowl; mix well. Store in an airtight container for up to 6 months.

STEAK SEASONING

YIELD: 1½ CUPS (288 G)

This is a great steak rub or seasoning. It's best to apply this to meat 30 minutes prior to cooking.

½ cup (125 g) kosher salt

½ cup (80 g) granulated garlic

¼ cup (55 g) turbinado sugar

¼ cup (28 g) ground black pepper, café grind (see page 153)

Add the salt, garlic, sugar and black pepper to a small bowl; mix well. Store in an airtight container for up to 6 months.

RIB RUB

YIELD: 3½ CUPS (660 G)

This rub is simple and will give flavor to all varieties of pork ribs. Rub liberally on the meat side of ribs.

1 cup (250 g) kosher salt

1 cup (220 g) turbinado sugar

½ cup (80 g) granulated garlic

½ cup (55 g) ground black pepper, café grind (see page 153)

2 tbsp (16 g) chili powder

1 tbsp (3 g) dried thyme

2 tbsp (14 g) granulated onion powder

3 tbsp (20 g) paprika

Add the salt, sugar, garlic, pepper, chili powder, thyme, onion powder and paprika to a small bowl; mix well. Store in an airtight container for up to 6 months.

COFFEE RUB

YIELD: 1 CUP (165 G)

A savory blend, this rub tastes great on steaks, hamburgers and beef ribs.

½ cup (125 g) kosher salt

3 tbsp (9 g) dark roast ground coffee

2 tbsp (14 g) coarsely ground pepper

1 tbsp (14 g) turbinado sugar

½ tsp chili powder

½ tsp cocoa powder

Add the salt, coffee, pepper, sugar, chili powder and cocoa powder to a small bowl; mix well. Store in an airtight container for up to 6 months.

SEAFOOD RUB

YIELD: 2 CUPS (235 G)

I am a fan of simple and easy. Fresh seafood is the best, and with this rub we try to showcase the depth of flavor in our dish and not overpower it. We want every bite to have the same flavor and depth to which you are accustomed. This rub is fabulous on shrimp and salmon. We also use it when we make a low-country boil.

⅓ cup (88 g) coarse flake salt

⅓ cup (36 g) paprika

¼ cup (39 g) garlic powder

¼ cup (28 g) freshly ground pepper

2 tbsp (5 g) dried thyme

2 tbsp (7 g) dried rosemary

2 tbsp (16 g) ground chipotle pepper

2 tbsp (14 g) onion powder

Add the salt, paprika, garlic, pepper, thyme, rosemary, chipotle pepper and onion to a small bowl; mix well. Store in an airtight container for up to 6 months.

TRADITIONAL BBQ SAUCE

YIELD: 3 CUPS (720 ML)

This is a great sauce recipe to use on beef, ribs and poultry. It is also a starting point for dreaming up your own sauce and flavor profiles. Get creative and feel free to try various combinations. If you like to bring the heat, introduce cayenne or chili powder to the recipe.

2 cups (480 ml) tomato ketchup

¼ cup (60 ml) apple cider vinegar

¼ cup (55 g) brown sugar

2 tbsp (30 g) yellow mustard

¼ cup (60 ml) honey

Combine the ketchup, vinegar, sugar, mustard and honey in a small bowl; mix well. Refrigerate the sauce until ready to use. Any unused sauce can be stored in a jar or airtight container in the refrigerator for 2 weeks.

CAROLINA VINEGAR SAUCE

YIELD: 2½ CUPS (600 ML)

This is a recipe straight out of the Piedmont Mountain region of the Carolinas. When you are talking Carolinas, you are talking about the whole hog. This recipe is great for pulled pork. It is also a great substitute for ketchup on French fries and will complement your pulled turkey sandwich as well.

2 tbsp (30 g) ketchup

2 cups (480 ml) apple cider vinegar

1 tbsp (15 ml) red hot sauce

1 tsp red pepper flakes

2 tbsp (28 g) brown sugar

Salt and pepper to taste

Add the ketchup, vinegar, hot sauce, pepper flakes, brown sugar, salt and pepper to a small pot over low heat; simmer for 10 minutes, stirring occasionally, until the sugar is dissolved. Strain the sauce and serve. Any unused sauce can be stored in a jar or airtight container in the refrigerator for 2 weeks.

WHITE BBQ SAUCE

YIELD: 3½ CUPS (830 ML)

White BBQ sauce, also known as Alabama White Sauce, is a tangy BBQ sauce with a kick. The White BBQ Sauce has found its home with all forms of poultry but we really love it with chicken. It can be used as a marinade or a dipping sauce. We like to take our BBQ chicken off the Traeger and dunk it in a bowl of White BBQ Sauce—it's tough to find a better balance than a chicken with white sauce.

2 cups (460 g) mayonnaise

1 cup (240 ml) white vinegar

¼ cup (60 ml) apple juice

1 tbsp (15 g) horseradish

1 tbsp (15 ml) lemon juice

1 tsp cayenne pepper

2 tsp (5 g) black pepper

In a large bowl, whisk together the mayonnaise, vinegar, apple juice, horseradish, lemon juice, cayenne pepper and black pepper until thoroughly combined. Store, refrigerated, for up to 2 weeks.

KOREAN BBQ SAUCE

YIELD: 1½ CUPS (360 ML)

Korean BBQ Sauce is not your traditional BBQ sauce. This is a sauce with a strong, deep, bold flavor profile. This is a great sauce for chicken and ribs. Yes, you heard me, ribs. Baby-back ribs with Korean BBQ Sauce make for a great cocktail party or appetizer item for your guests.

½ cup (120 ml) gochujang

¼ cup (60 ml) soy sauce

¼ cup (60 ml) mirin/rice wine

2 tbsp (30 ml) sesame oil

1 tbsp (8 g) gochugaru

¼ cup (60 ml) honey

¼ cup (60 ml) water

In a large bowl, whisk together the gochujang, soy sauce, mirin, sesame oil, gochugaru, honey and water until thoroughly combined. Store, refrigerated, for up to 2 weeks.

MUSTARD SAUCE

YIELD: 2 CUPS (480 ML)

If you have had the pleasure of traveling to South Carolina, you will know about mustard sauce. That is where I came up with my inspiration for our mustard sauce; however, I decided to add some brown sugar to sweeten up the traditional flavor. This recipe can be used as a sauce, marinade or dressing. We have used it on everything from poultry to lamb chops to salads.

1 cup (230 g) yellow mustard

½ cup (120 ml) honey

¼ cup (60 ml) apple cider vinegar

2 tbsp (30 ml) ketchup

1 tbsp (14 g) brown sugar

3 tbsp (45 ml) Worcestershire sauce

In a small bowl, mix the mustard, honey, vinegar, ketchup, brown sugar and Worcestershire sauce until combined. This sauce is best if it is made the day before you plan to use it and then refrigerated. Store, refrigerated, for up to 2 weeks.

SPICES AND THEIR USES

It wasn't until I started to really dive into the world of BBQ that I became particular about which spices I used. Ultimately, spices are the base of your flavor; they are the foundation. Like most of you, our pantry is filled with random jars and containers of spices, and we usually cannot remember when we purchased any of them. That is a bad thing, very bad. There is a distinctive difference in the flavor and performance of spices that are old. I am not telling you to clean out your pantry and dump everything; however, if the spice isn't fragrant, it might be time to buy a replacement. The same can be said for spices in your local grocery store as well and most definitely at the big box stores. How can they sell such a large quantity container so inexpensively? Because they are not using top-quality spices. At home, I suggest keeping a fairly small quantity of your spices, making sure they are stored in a cool, dark space. A rule of thumb is to replace them at least once a year, or whenever they start to lose their color or freshness. Try to find yourself a spice purveyor you know has consistent and high-quality products. Personally, I really like Penzeys Spices.

Here's a rundown of some essential BBQ spices:

Aleppo pepper—A robust, bright-red pepper found in a lot of Mediterranean dishes; Aleppo pepper is somewhat similar to ancho chile powder but with a bit more of a punch of robust flavor that dissipates quickly.

Ancho chile powder—Made from ground poblano peppers, ancho chile powder is dark and smoky, with a deep, rich flavor and mild heat. We love it and think it is the perfect powder for those looking for a milder taste in their food.

Cayenne pepper— This seasoning is a finely ground powder prepared from the seeds and pods of various types of chiles. The powder is a reddish-brown color and has some heat behind it. Cayenne pepper is an instant blood-flow stimulant, promoting circulation so blood can carry other nutrients to cells more efficiently.

Chinese five spice—This blend is a staple in Chinese cooking. Typically made up of star anise, cloves, cinnamon, Szechuan pepper and fennel seeds, it is dominated by the aroma and flavor of star anise. Add a little salt and it is an excellent rub for chicken.

Cumin—Used in a wide range of dishes, mainly where highly spiced foods are preferred, cumin is a common ingredient in Middle Eastern, Spanish and Mexican dishes. It has a strong, spicy-sweet aroma with a powerful and sharp flavor.

Garlic—The bulb of a lily-like plant belonging to the same family as the onion, chive, leek and scallion, garlic has infinite uses and is an important ingredient in the dishes of most cuisines. I like to use the granulated variety for our rubs.

Old Bay seasoning—This spice mix is a must-have for low-country boils and other seafood dishes.

Paprika—Made from red peppers that are larger and milder than chile peppers, paprika is an ideal spice for BBQ rubs as it adds vibrant color with a nominal effect on your taste profile. The color is a striking deep red that spreads through any dish to which it is added.

Pepper—Pepper is a staple in nearly every dish, and we use the café/restaurant mesh grind for all of our rubs. The grind size is important. Too thick and it will be gritty; too thin and it will be pasty. As you become more familiar and adventurous with your rubs, it is the slightest changes that can have a profound effect on your end product.

Rosemary—With its distinctive, strong flavor, rosemary convinces your taste buds that herbs are not just delicate items made to enhance a side dish. Rosemary is a take-charge herb with a woodsy yet mint-like finish. It is great for all red meats.

Salt—We always use kosher salt unless otherwise directed.

Thyme—With an aroma and taste that is warming, fresh and agreeable, thyme is widely used and works well with a variety of red meat dishes, as well as for seafood, soups, stocks and aiolis. I like to use thyme when I use rosemary to help balance out the profoundness of the rosemary.

TOOLS OF THE TRADE

There are many elements to take into account in order to achieve good barbecue. The two most important factors to me are your equipment and your tools. Your Traeger grill will provide you with clean, consistent cooks, so if you have a Traeger you are well equipped. Now let's focus on the tools needed to maintain your elite pitmaster status:

Basting brush or mop—I prefer silicone basting brushes. They are durable and can be used either to baste or sauce your meat and will never shed.

Cotton gloves and disposable gloves—Rarely will I use the Traeger grill without wearing gloves. The cotton gloves are great for insulating your hands from the heat. Put a pair of cotton gloves on first and then a pair of disposable gloves over them and you will be handling the hot stuff with ease.

Digital instant-read thermometer—This is a must-have tool for cooking on a Traeger, or any grill for that matter. Accurate and instant are both a necessity when you should be cookin' and not lookin'.

Disposable cutting boards—If you are someone like me who enjoys spending time outdoors and is afraid to make a mess inside, get yourself a pack of disposable cutting boards. Disposable cutting boards are really helpful for avoiding cross-contamination. They are made of a high-quality, coated, food-grade paper. They have a large cutting area of 18 x 24 inches (46 x 61 cm), but can be cut to size for smaller jobs. These can be found at various online retailers.

Disposable half-size aluminum trays—Do yourself a favor and buy a case of these from your local restaurant supply store. From transporting raw meat to keeping your finished product hot, you will always find yourself looking for a clean tray to use.

Grill brush—Use one to keep the grate clean in between cooks.

Injector—This is the tool to use when you get brave and decide you want to try to inject large cuts of meat for additional flavor. I recommend an injector with large needles so you can penetrate the thickness of the meat.

Shakers/dredge—Use these to help you evenly apply rubs and seasonings to meat.

Tongs and spatulas—These are familiar to all kitchens and home cooks; however, for barbecue, you will want to find long-handled versions for safely handling larger cuts of meat.

BASIC KITCHEN SANITATION

A basic refresher on sanitation is a must if you are going to be cooking, BBQing or cutting meat and poultry at home.

The #1 most important rule is: Wash your hands and equipment frequently with hot water and soap. I also like to use a hand sanitizer before and after coming in contact with meat, poultry and vegetables. You don't need a lot; a drop the size of a dime is enough. Then, rub it on your hands until they are dry (approximately twenty seconds). Those twenty seconds kill 99.9 percent of the most common germs, which is a worthwhile use of time.

I also recommend using food-safe gloves when handling meat. Make sure to buy the gloves with no powder. Personally I recommend and prefer nitrile gloves. These can be purchased in quantity at a reasonable price online and in most big box stores.

The next area of concern is cross-contamination in your food-prep area. Proper cleaning procedures and common sense prevail here and will prevent you, your family and your guests from any unpleasant food bacteria–related illness. I can't stress this enough. I suggest using a different cutting board for your three main categories of food prep: one for meats, one for poultry and one for cutting fresh vegetables. I like to buy my cutting boards color-coded—red for meat, yellow for poultry and green for vegetables. It's also good to make sure your cutting boards are NSF approved. Whatever you do, clean those properly after each use and you should not have any problems. Wash your boards in hot soapy water, making sure to loosen any meat particles stuck to the surface with a brush, then rinse in hot water. Now make a sanitizing solution of bleach and cold water (hot water will kill the sanitizing benefits of bleach). I recommend using a ratio of 1 ounce (30 ml) of bleach per gallon (3.8 L) of water. Wipe down the board thoroughly with the sanitizer solution. Then rinse the board thoroughly and let it air dry. Before each use, I suggest dipping a paper towel in a fresh solution of the bleach/water mixture and wiping the cutting board to make sure to kill any airborne germs that may have accrued during storage.

Follow the procedure above with any other equipment or surfaces that came in contact with the meat. Wipe your knives dry as soon as you have finished sanitizing them, as bleach may stain or even rust certain metal knives.

ACKNOWLEDGMENTS

To be asked to author one cookbook is an honor; a second one is a privilege. It is an opportunity to share what I know about barbecue so readers can share with their families and friends. But to me this book and even my Handsome Devil brand wouldn't be possible without the support, hard work and dedication of so many others.

First and foremost, I thank my wife, Noelle Randolph, who is the real reason any of this has happened and the most vital part of everything I am. She has been through it all, patiently letting me chase my dream. I can always trust her to give me an honest opinion on the recipes. She made this book better.

To my parents, Joan and Ed Randolph. Thank you for inspiring me and enriching me with values and pride. I love you.

To my grandparents, John and Helen Randolph. I wouldn't be in business if it weren't for you. You instilled my life with traditions, independence and the love of feeding and supporting people. I hope you can look down and be proud of what we have accomplished. To this day I can hear my grandfather tell me, "Edward, there will be a time in your life you won't have the biggest house, nicest car or prettiest clothes, but one thing no one can ever take from you is your pride. Work hard and be proud at the end of the day." P.S. Grandma, I didn't eat the 2 pounds of bacon—it was Steve.

Anyone who has ever met Ken Goodman knows that I can say "friend" with pride. And if you ask Ken, he would probably say that we are not friends—we are family. He is a world-class photographer and has captured images of some of the most iconic chefs. I am blessed to have worked with Ken twice now, and his photos are just an extension of who he is. His photos are full of life, love and happiness. Ken has made me a better man. Love ya, brother. I can't thank you enough for all you do.

I couldn't have done this without the unfailing support and guidance of Page Street Publishing. Special thanks to Will Kiester and Marissa Giambelluca for giving me the opportunity to showcase some of my fun behind the grill. I can't forget Karen Levy and Simone Payment, who worked behind the scenes organizing and assisting with this book.

Huge thanks to all of the pitmasters, chefs and barbecue fanatics who I can truly call friends. You have always supported me and never wavered on giving me advice or some of your house secrets. I can't mention one without mentioning everyone, and that would take up another chapter. Thank you all.

A debt of gratitude goes to the entire staff of Handsome Devil LLC. Their hard work and dedication gave me the opportunity to write a second book. It is an accomplishment we should all be proud of.

Thank you to my daughters, Lily, Emma and Amai, three beautiful young women with the world in the palm of their hand. Your love and smiles motivate me to do more. "As long as one and one is two, there couldn't be a father who loves his daughters more than I love you."

Last, thank you! Yes, you, the one reading this book right now. Every time you visit us, recommend us to others, like a picture on social media, write a comment or share one of our posts, you are supporting our small family business and we appreciate you. Eat local. Shop local. Buy local.

LIVE. LOVE. EAT BBQ.

ABOUT THE AUTHOR

Ed Randolph is the founder, owner and pitmaster of Handsome Devil LLC. Randolph and Handsome Devil LLC received national attention when they won the Food Network's 2017 New York Wine & Food Festival for Best BBQ. He is also the author of *Smoked: One Man's Journey to Find Incredible Recipes, Standout Pitmasters and the Stories Behind Them.* Randolph appeared on—and won—Food Network's *Chopped* in 2019.

Randolph, who grew up in the farming-rich area of Hudson Valley, New York, absorbed cooking techniques from his Italian mother and Polish grandmother. Randolph's ambitious, all-hustle approach has taken the Handsome Devil brand from the rural backwoods to the bright lights of Broadway. Appearing at more than 50 events a season, the Handsome Devil team has traveled from Vermont to Florida to compete and share their BBQ with the public. In 2014, the Handsome Devil team was recognized by the BBQ community for their efforts and invited to be the BBQ vendor for the Memphis in May World BBQ Championships in Memphis, Tennessee. It was the first time anyone from New York had been asked to attend. In addition to the Food Network championship, the Handsome Devil team has amassed state championship awards in six states; catered events for numerous Fortune 500 companies and movie premieres for Warner Brothers; and catered high-profile events such as the New York Airshow, the Taste of Country Music Festival and numerous Beer, Bourbon and BBQ festivals.

Randolph currently resides in Newburgh, New York, with his wife, Noelle, and daughters Lily, Emma and Amai. As a small business owner, Randolph understands the importance of community. He is a contributor to Operation BBQ Relief, local veterans and youth organizations and Beyond Type 1. He also enjoys auto racing with his Higbie Family Race team.

INDEX